Roderick Chisholm has bee[...] important and influential p[...] [...]g to metaphysics, philosophy of mind, and epistemology. This book can be viewed as a summation of his views on an enormous range of topics in metaphysics and epistemology. Yet it is written in the terse, lucid, unpretentious style that has become a hallmark of Chisholm's work.

The book is a treatise designed to defend an original, non-Aristotelian theory of categories. Chisholm argues that there are necessary things and contingent things, necessary things being things that are not capable of coming into being or passing away. He defends the argument from design and thus includes the category of necessary substance (God). Further contentions of the essay are that attributes are also necessary beings, that there are no such entities as "times," and that human beings are contingent substances but may not be material substances.

A REALISTIC THEORY OF CATEGORIES

A Realistic Theory of Categories

An Essay on Ontology

RODERICK M. CHISHOLM
Brown University

CAMBRIDGE
UNIVERSITY PRESS

CAMBRIDGE UNIVERSITY PRESS
Cambridge, New York, Melbourne, Madrid, Cape Town, Singapore, São Paulo

Cambridge University Press
The Edinburgh Building, Cambridge CB2 8RU, UK

Published in the United States of America by Cambridge University Press, New York

www.cambridge.org
Information on this title: www.cambridge.org/9780521554268

First published 1996

A catalogue record for this publication is available from the British Library

Library of Congress Cataloguing in Publication data
Chisholm, Roderick M.
A realistic theory of categories : an essay on ontology / Roderick M.
Chisholm.
p.   cm.
Includes index.
ISBN 0-521-55426-8. – ISBN 0-521-55616-3 (pbk.)
1. Ontology.   2. Categories (Philosophy)   3. Realism.   I. Title.
B945.C463R42   1996
111 – dc20   95-39427
                                                                CIP

ISBN 978-0-521-55426-8 hardback
ISBN 978-0-521-55616-3 paperback

Transferred to digital printing 2007

Dedicated to my wife Eleanor

CONTENTS

Contents

ACKNOWLEDGMENTS

I HERE express my thanks to the many people who have helped to make this book possible.

I thank the publishers who have given me permission to quote from other authors. I also express my indebtedness to Ms Louise Calabro from Cambridge University Press. I thank the philosophers who read and commented on earlier versions of the manuscript. These include Dr. Johann C. Marek of the University of Graz, who read a preliminary version; the publisher's readers; and Mr. Matthew McGrath, a graduate student at Brown University, who went through the book with great care and made devastating objections to fundamental points. Or, rather, the objections would have been devastating if he had not answered them for me. They made me see the whole subject in a clearer light. Consequently, the book is a great improvement over what might have been. I am responsible for any errors that remain.

I am indebted to the Officers of Administration and to the Department of Philosophy of Brown University for making it possible for me to practice philosophy under ideal conditions. I single out, in particular, Ernest Sosa, who has been especially helpful to me during our long association at Brown.

I wish also to thank my son, Jonathan Chisholm, and Dr. Allen Renear of Brown for their help in enabling me to produce the manuscript on Brown's mainframe computer.

Above all I thank my wife. This book is dedicated to her.

Roderick M. Chisholm

PART ONE

The Realistic Background

1

INTRODUCTION

WHAT IS THE THEORY OF CATEGORIES?

This book is about the ultimate categories of reality. It is about *categories*, not about *theories of categories*. What a category is may be shown by depicting the table of categories that is defended here.

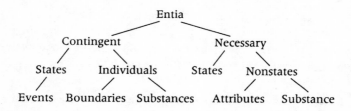

A Table of Categories

It was Aristotle who first worked out a theory of categories. But the general procedure that I will follow is not the one that Aristotle followed in his treatise on the subject. And the theory that I defend rejects many of the metaphysical views that are generally associated with Aristotle: for example, the doctrine of form and matter, the distinction between substance and accident, and the "moderate realism" according to which the only attributes that exist are those that are exemplified. Nevertheless, I will follow Aristotle and will make use of his insights throughout this book.[1]

3

THE NATURE OF THE PRESENT THEORY

The present theory is "Platonistic": it is a form of *extreme realism*. There are *attributes* (properties). Some of them (e.g., being a dog) are exemplified; some of them (e.g., being a unicorn) are unexemplified; and some of them (e.g., being a round square) cannot be exemplified. Classes or sets may be reduced to attributes, and relations may be reduced to classes or sets.

There are *substances* and there are *events*. Neither can be defined in terms of the other. Substances are individuals that are not boundaries. Events are contingent states. Material things are substances and persons are substances. But it is problematic whether persons are material things.

What philosophers call *times* will be shown to be dispensable. There are good reasons for rejecting the view that events are constructs out of attributes and times. Statements such as "He has done that seven times" are reducible to tensed statements that do not ostensibly refer to times but only to temporal relations.

Places are reducible to the individuals that may be said to occupy those places. More exactly, statements ostensibly about places may be reduced to statements ostensibly about individual things and the spatial relations that hold among those things.

Appearances, visual and otherwise, are surfaces that give reality a qualitative dimension. (Hence the adverbial theory of appearances is rejected.)

Our approach to philosophy is what Charles Sanders Peirce has called "critical commonsensism." This approach is based on faith in one's own rationality. Reason, as Peirce put it, not only corrects its premises, "it also corrects its own conclusions."[2]

We thus rely, albeit somewhat cautiously, on perception, both inner and outer. I assume that our perception of our own states of mind is a source of certainty and that the deliverances of external perception should be treated as innocent, epistemically, unless we have positive reason to call them into question. We may thus be said to presuppose a *realistic* theory of knowledge.

The remainder of this chapter is concerned with methodological questions. The actual development of a theory of categories begins in the following chapter.

THE BASIC CATEGORIAL CONCEPTS

The present theory, like any other, makes use of certain concepts that are distinctly philosophical. And, like any other philosophical theory, it takes certain philosophical concepts as undefined. In setting forth the theory of categories itself, the core of this book, I use eight such undefined concepts. Three of them are *ontological*; one is *intentional*; one is *psychological* but not intentional; one is *temporal*; one is *spatial*; and one is *nomological*, pertaining to laws of nature. I also use an ordinary vocabulary that is common to most investigators. This vocabulary includes familiar expressions of elementary *logic*.

The undefined categorial vocabulary here referred to pertains to the concepts that are depicted in the table of categories that I have set forth. Additional terms will be needed for other topics to be discussed in this book – for example, the theory of reference and the question of the primacy of the intentional.

We now consider the eight undefined categorial concepts. Axioms for these concepts will be introduced at appropriate places.

(1) The first undefined categorial locution is "x is necessarily such that it is F." The relevant sense of "necessarily" is here *logical* (or *metaphysical*) and not *causal*. Since even "logically necessary" may be used in different ways in philosophy, it is important to single out the principles that govern its present use. These may be put somewhat informally as follows. The

schematic letter "F" in "x is necessarily such that it is F" may be replaced only by a predicate expression in which no variables occur freely. The usual rules relating "necessarily" and "possibly" should apply; thus, "necessarily" implies "possibly," "not possibly not" implies "necessarily," and "not necessarily not" implies "possibly."[3]

(2)   The second undefined categorial concept is that of being a *state* – being a thing that is a *state of* another thing. If you are thinking, then there is a state that is you thinking. States are terms of the temporal relations of before and after, and terms of the relation of causation.

(3)   The third undefined categorial concept is that of being a *constituent* of another thing. Contingent things that are not states, and are therefore *individuals*, may be divided into (a) those that are necessarily such that they are constituents and (b) those that need not be constituents. (It is convenient to construe being a *part of* as a subspecies of being a *constituent of;* parts may then be said to be those constituents that are not boundaries.)

(4)   The fourth undefined categorial concept is the intentional concept of *believing*. In the following chapter on the nature of attributes, we define the concept of an attribute by reference, in part, to the *content* of an act of believing. (In discussing intentionality we assume, with Descartes and Brentano, that one cannot *believe that something is F* without thereby *thinking about something being F*. In other words, one cannot have anything as the *content of a belief* without having that same thing as a *content of an act of thought*.)

(5)   The fifth undefined categorial concept is *psychological* but not intentional. I express it by means of "x senses y." In saying that the attribute of sensing is psychological, I mean that it can be exemplified only by that which is capable of thinking. And in saying that sensing is not intentional, I mean this: The locu-

tion "a senses b," when it is used to express this concept, implies: "There exists an x and there exists a y, such that x senses y." We consider this concept in detail in Chapter 13.

(6) The sixth undefined categorial concept is a *temporal concept*. This is the relation of *wholly preceding* a transitive and asymmetrical relation between states. We follow Russell, who has shown how other temporal relations may be defined in terms of that of wholly preceding.

(7) The seventh undefined categorial concept is a *spatial* concept: "x *spatially overlaps* with y." Two rectangular boards, so located that one is on top of the other, may take the approximate form of an "I" or an "L" or a "T" or an "X" or a "Y." This concept of overlapping is used to throw light on the spatial nature of material things and on the distinction between such things and the boundaries that they contain (surfaces, lines, and points).

(8) Finally, I make use of a *nomological* concept, to be expressed by means of the locution "It is a law of nature that p," where the schematic letter "p" may be replaced by any well-formed declarative English sentence. In Chapter 10, I argue that causation is a nomological concept, a concept pertaining to the *laws of nature*, and that the laws of nature cannot be reduced to mere Humean regularities or "constant conjunctions."

Our eight undefined categorial locutions, then, are the following:

(1) x is necessarily such that it is F;
(2) x is a state of y;
(3) x is a constituent of y;
(4) x believes that something is F;
(5) x senses y;

(6) x wholly precedes y;
(7) x spatially overlaps with y;
(8) it is a law of nature that p.

In addition to making use of these eight undefined locutions, this analysis makes use of a language in which there are distinctions of *tense*. There is thus a distinction between "x is F," "x was F," and "x will be F."

Theories of categories, it is sometimes said, may be divided into those that are *substance philosophies* and those that are *process philosophies*. The former find no place for events or processes among the ultimate constituents of the world; the latter find no place for processes or events. The present theory finds a place for both.[4]

THE RELEVANCE OF LANGUAGE TO THE THEORY
OF CATEGORIES

Aristotle says that in discussing the categories, he is concerned in part with our ordinary language. And he says this often enough to provide encouragement to those contemporary philosophers who believe that the statements of metaphysicians, to the extent that they are not completely empty, tell us something about our language. One of our principal concerns, however, is that of finding the *ontological presuppositions* of statements about language.

Where some readers of this book may expect to find discussions of language, they will find discussions of thinking and intentionality instead. But this does not mean that I underestimate the fundamental role that language should have in serious philosophy.

I have begun by singling out those categorial concepts that are taken as undefined. Next, the additional concepts that are needed will be introduced in a series of definitions. These definitions embody the principal results of our investigations, and they tell us what we are ontologically committed to. Like the critical commonsensism that we assume preanalytically, the definitions are intended to guarantee that our results will be falsifiable.

We now turn to the theory of categories, beginning with an intentional account of the concept of a property or attribute.

2

THE NATURE OF ATTRIBUTES

INTRODUCTION

The present theory of attributes is, as already mentioned, a version of Platonism. There are attributes. Some are exemplified; some are not; and some cannot be.

To the skeptical reader, I would first point out that someone should try to work out the consequences of such an ontology. There seem to be no available examples. I would add, moreover, that our apparent extravagance here enables us to achieve a compensating parsimony elsewhere – for example, in connection with those entities that are called *propositions*.

THE CONCEPT OF AN ATTRIBUTE DEFINED

We begin with the concept of the *content* of an act of believing.

> D1 x has being-F as the content of an act of
> believing =Df (1) x believes that there is a
> y such that y is F; and (2) x does not be-
> lieve that there is anything that is F if and
> only if it is not F

I shall comment presently on clause (2), which is inserted to avoid the consequences of Russell's paradox.

The reference to *believing* in clause (1) may be replaced by a reference to any other intentional attitude – for example, *considering* and *endeavoring*. I assume, with Descartes, that every such attitude implies the attitude of *thinking*. Hence "an act of thinking" may replace "an act of believing" in this definition.

11

> D2   x exemplifies being-F =Df (1) Being-F is
> possibly such that it is the content of an
> act of believing; and (2) x is F

The present uses of "being-F" and of "F" may be explicated as
follows. The letter "F" is a predicate schema that may be replaced by any English predicate (e.g., by "green"). When "F"
is replaced in "being-F," then the result is a *term*. In the definitions that immediately follow, "being-F" occurs in contexts
that are subject to quantification. "Being green is exemplified
by many leaves," for example, implies "There *exists* an x such
that x is exemplified by many leaves."

> D3   Being-F is an attribute =Df Being-F is pos-
> sibly such that it is the content of an act
> of believing

> D4   P conceptually entails Q =Df P and Q are
> necessarily such that whoever has P as the
> content of an act of believing also has Q as
> the content of an act of believing

ATTRIBUTES AND RUSSELL'S PARADOX

Russell's paradox arises in connection with the class of all
classes that are not members of themselves. If we say that that
class *is* a member of itself, then our statement implies that it is
not a member of itself. And if we say that it is *not* a member of
itself, then our statement implies that it *is* a member of itself.

Here we follow Quine's proposal for dealing with such para-
doxes. He summarizes his conclusions this way:

> All these antinomies and other related cases may be inactivated
> by limiting the guilty principle of class membership in a very
> simple way. The principle is that for any membership condition
> you can formulate there is a class whose members are solely
> the things meeting the condition. We get Russell's antinomy
> and all the others of its series by taking the condition as non-
> membership in self, or non-membership in members of self,

and the like. . . . If we withhold our principle of class existence from cases where the membership condition mentions membership, Russell's antinomy and related ones are no longer forthcoming.[1]

The proposal is, in short, to treat the problematic attribute the way one treats the problem of the barber who shaves all and only those men who do not shave themselves. Does he shave himself? One denies that there *is* such a barber, thereby avoiding the question of whether he shaves himself.

THE EXTENSIONAL CRITERION OF THE IDENTITY OF ATTRIBUTES

There is a relatively simple extensional criterion for the identity of *sets* or *classes:* Sets or classes are identical provided only that they have the same members. That is to say, class A is identical to class B if and only if whatever is a member of A is a member of B and conversely. But we cannot apply this criterion to the identity of attributes.

According to one traditional example, adoption of such a criterion would have the consequence that the attribute of being a rational animal is identical to the attribute of being a featherless biped. According to another traditional example, such a criterion would have the consequence that the attribute of having a sense of humor is identical to that of being a rational animal. The criterion would also have the consequence that the attribute of being a unicorn is identical to that of being a mermaid.

DEFENSE OF AN INTENTIONAL CRITERION

But we may formulate an *intentional* criterion of attribute identity, making use of the concept of *conceptual entailment*, defined in definition D4.

(C1)   Attribute A is identical to attribute B =Df
       Attributes A and B are necessarily so re-
       lated that whoever has one as intentional
       content of an act of thought has the other
       as intentional content of an act of thought

This criterion does not have the difficulties of the one just considered. Nor does it require us to say that the attribute of being a rational animal is identical to that of being a featherless biped, and it does not require us to say that the attribute of being a mermaid is identical to the attribute of being a round square.

To make the present criterion clear, we consider two possible objections, (A) and (B).

Objection (A): Suppose that John believes Mary to be pretty. The word *pretty*, in this use, is synonymous with *pulchritudinous*. Therefore, the attributes of being pretty and being pulchritudinous are necessarily so related that whoever attributes the one also attributes the other. But John has no idea of what *pulchritudinous* means; and if we asked him whether it applied to Mary, he could say, quite sincerely, "Not as far as I know." Therefore, although John believes that Mary is pretty, he does not believe that she is pulchritudinous. Hence (the objector concludes), the intentional criterion of attribute identity is inadequate.

The reply is that from the fact that John does not believe that the word *pulchritudinous* applies to Mary, it does follow that John does not believe that Mary is pulchritudinous. Analogously, one who knew no English might well believe that Mary is pretty without knowing that *pretty* applies to Mary.

Objection (B) is somewhat more complex.[2] It may be formulated as follows:

(1)   There is a person S who can truly say, "Black is the color of my true love's hair."

14

Therefore:

(2) The following attributes are identical: (a) black and (b) the color of the true love's hair.

(3) According to C1, the identity criterion for attributes, the two attributes are distinct. One can attribute either of them without thereby attributing the other.

Hence:

(4) The criterion of attribute identity is inadequate.

It is essential to be sensitive to the language we use when discussing philosophical problems. Some philosophers believe that it is advisable to construct an "ideal" language to deal with such problems. I suggest, however, that it is sufficient to refine our ordinary language.

In English and apparently in most Western languages, color adjectives such as *black* also function as nouns, as when we say "Black is a color that is not chromatic." Other types of adjectives – for example, *unruly* and *unkempt* – occasionally function as nouns but, except where the words are being used as names for themselves, the results are unnatural and strained.

In formulating D1, the intentional definition of the concept of an attribute, I have said that the locution "x believes that something is F" should be so interpreted that the letter "F" is replaceable only by predicate expressions and that it should not be replaced by singular terms – that is, by names or definite descriptions.

Our problems arise from the ambiguity, already referred to, in the ordinary use of the verb *is*. Sometimes we use it as the "is" of predication, in which case it is properly followed only by an adjectival expression. And sometimes we use it in a quite different way – as the "is" of identity; in this case, it properly falls between singular terms. I suggest that for our present purpose only, we formulate the problem by replacing the "is" of identity by the identity sign (=), an expression in which the verb *is* does not appear at all. When we do this, we will restrict *is* to its predicative use.[3] And when we use adjectives as names, we will capitalize them, as one does in German.

Now we may reformulate the attributions in question:

(1) My true love's hair is black.
(2) The color of my true love's hair = Black.

Given the assumptions of our example, we may say that the following attributes are identical: (a) Black and (b) the color of the true love's hair.[4]

Given D1, we may affirm:

> A1   For every x, being-F is attributed by x if
> and only if x believes that something is F

Relying on the identity of being-black and Black, we replace "being-F" in the first clause by "Black" and replace "F" in the final clause by "black," and so obtain the following as a consequence of an instantiation of A1:

> A1'   For every x, Black is attributed by x if and
> only if x believes that there is something
> that is black

Given the identity of Black and the color of my true love's hair, together with A1', we have the following:

> For every x, the color of my true love's
> hair is attributed by x if and only if x be-
> lieves that something is black

Returning now to Objection (2), we see that the third step does not follow from those that precede it. Our criterion (C1) of the identity of attributes does not have the consequence that the attributes (a) and (b) are distinct. And, given our analysis, we may say that (a) and (b) are one and the same. Therefore, the objection does not show that the intentional criterion of the identity of attributes is inadequate.

The considerations presented, therefore, do not constitute a difficulty for the intentional criterion.

We consider an additional objection in the following chapter, where we discuss in more detail the relation between sets and attributes.

THE FIRST DICHOTOMY

We define *contingent* things as things that are not necessary. And since, according to our ontology, all attributes are necessary things, we may, without circularity, define necessary things in terms of attributes. But we do not say that a necessary thing is a thing that exists necessarily.

This would violate the conditions on the use of *necessarily* that we set forth in Chapter 1. We said that *necessarily* is to be used only in expressions of the form "x is necessarily such that it is F," where the schematic letter "F" is to be replaced only by a predicate.

We will say this instead:

> D5   x is a necessary thing (an *ens necessa-rium*) =Df There is an attribute that is such that (1) everything is necessarily such that there is something having that attribute, (2) x is necessarily such that it has that attribute, and (3) that attribute is not necessarily had by everything

For example, the necessary thing that is the attribute being-green has the following attribute necessarily: being such that it is exemplified only if something is green. And *everything* is necessarily such that something has that attribute.

> D6   x is a contingent thing =Df x is a thing that is not a necessary thing

But, one may now object, you don't even have a proper dichotomy here. For there are some things that are neither nec-

17

essary nor contingent – namely, *impossible things* such as the attribute of being a round square. Your first dichotomy, which appears to divide all things into two exclusive classes, has no place for such things.

One way of drawing the distinction between necessary things and contingent things is set forth in Chapter 9. The distinction is essentially this: A contingent thing is a thing that could have come into being or could pass away, and a necessary thing is a thing that could not have come into being and cannot pass away. The concepts of *coming into being* and *passing away* are discussed in Chapter 9,[5] but we shall draw the distinction in another way here.

We note, first, that there are *no* impossible things. There are attributes that philosophers may refer to, somewhat misleadingly, as impossible attributes. But an impossible attribute – say, being a round square – is not an attribute that *cannot exist*. It is an attribute that *cannot be exemplified*. Everything is necessarily such that there is an attribute such that, if anything has it, then something is both round and square. In other words, there exists an attribute, which is that of being both round and square, and that attribute is necessarily such that either nothing has it or something is both round and square. Hence our first dichotomy, that between necessary things and contingent things, divides all things into two exclusive classes.

In the following chapter, I provide additional assurance that there *are* attributes that are not exemplified.

3

THE EXISTENCE OF ATTRIBUTES

INTRODUCTION

According to what we have been saying, if you believe that there are dogs, then being a dog is the content of that state that is you believing that there are dogs. But this account does not yield anything like a proof of the thesis according to which there is such a thing as the attribute of being a dog.

Here I set forth an independent philosophical argument for the thesis according to which there are attributes. What I say does not purport to be a demonstration or proof, but it does offer a good reason for its conclusion. The argument has three steps.

(1) We formulate a criterion of ontological commitment, which spells out some of the circumstances that commit us to the belief that there are attributes. (2) We then consider a number of ostensible ways of showing that we are thus committed. We reject some of these, and we withhold commitment – at least provisionally – with respect to others. And finally (3), we set forth a type of consideration that does yield a good reason for believing that there *are* attributes – a good reason for believing not only that there are such attributes as that of being a dog, which are *exemplified,* but also a good reason for believing that there are attributes such as that of being a winged horse, that are *not exemplified,* and for believing that there are attributes such as that of being a round square, which *cannot be exemplified.*

A CRITERION OF ONTOLOGICAL COMMITMENT

How do we decide whether there are such entities as attributes? We should remind ourselves that having a good reason for a belief is not the same as being able to *prove logically* that what is thus believed is true.

Our criterion tells us that under the following circumstances, we would have a good reason for believing that there are attributes.

(1) We consider a belief for which we do have a good reason. (2) We find that the belief can be adequately expressed in statements (a) that contain terms purporting to designate attributes and (b) that these terms in that use are subject to existential generalization. And finally, (3) we find that we cannot express the belief in question without using terms that thus purport to designate attributes.[1]

If these conditions are fulfilled, then the belief is one that commits us to believing that there are attributes or properties. And then we have a good reason for believing that there are such entities.

A PROBLEMATIC CASE

To see how the present criterion of ontological commitment is to be applied, we consider several different examples.

Consider "Dogness (canininity) is well represented in Rhode Island." The statement tells us that there are many dogs in Rhode Island. Therefore, our first condition of the criterion is fulfilled; the statement expresses something that some of us have good reason to believe. It also fulfills the second condition, for it uses a term (*dogness* or *canininity*) that purports to designate dogness. But does it fulfill the third condition? Do we need to use abstract terms to say what the original statement expresses? The answer is no. For we may express the

20

statement in a way that does not use any abstract terms. We need say only "There are many dogs in Rhode Island."

In this case, therefore, we have reduced talk that is ostensibly about the attribute of canininity to talk that is not ostensibly about that attribute.

THE ARGUMENT FOR EXTREME REALISM

There are certain other truths that would seem to be truths about properties or attributes. And they appear to be incapable of paraphrase in statements that make no ostensible reference to properties or universals.

Consider such statements as

There are virtues that are not exemplified.

Diogenes was specific, saying, "Honesty is not exemplified." But we may be more cautious. "Perhaps courage is exemplified, perhaps genuine altruism is exemplified – but some virtues, surely, are not exemplified." How are we to put this fact without ostensibly referring to attributes? The question here, of course, does not concern the evidence for the assertion. It has to do with what is being said.

A less cynical example will also do:

There are vices that are not exemplified.

But we need not restrict ourselves to ethical examples. We may use similar examples from other spheres. Consider this highly plausible version of the argument:

There are types of automobiles that are not exemplified.

There are shapes that are not exemplified.

Can we put these truths in such a way that our statements make no ostensible reference to properties or attributes? I recommend that the reader try to construct such a paraphrase.

4

PROPOSITIONS AS REDUCIBLE TO ATTRIBUTES

INTRODUCTION

Philosophers standardly use the term *proposition* to describe "the referents of 'that'-clauses." One says, "'That Socrates is mortal' refers to the proposition that Socrates is mortal."

We may certainly speak as though there *are* propositions in this technical sense. But we do not need to say that there are propositions *in addition to* attributes. For talk ostensibly about propositions may be *reduced to* talk about attributes. Therefore propositions, unlike attributes, are not part of the "ultimate furniture" of the world.

Attributes perform whatever useful functions propositions perform. We shall see, moreover, that the assumption of a special category of propositions involves serious difficulties.

We presuppose what we have said about the nature of attributes: An *attribute* is anything that is possibly such that it is the content of an act of thinking.

In the definitions that follow, the schematic letter "p" may be replaced by any well-formed declarative English sentence.[1]

D1 The proposition that p is true =Df There is something that has the attribute of being such that p

D2 The proposition that q is the negation of the proposition that p =Df The attribute of being such that p is necessarily such that it is exemplified if and only if the attribute of being such that q is not exemplified

D3   The proposition that p is false =Df The negation of the proposition that p is true

D4   The proposition that p exists =df The attribute of being such that p exists.

Given our reduction of proposition-talk in terms of
attribute-talk, we may introduce a notion of propositions as
attributes of the form "being such that p." Our notion of proposition is a departure from the standard philosophical notion,
but is preferable insofar as it can be made to do all the same
essential work done by the standard notion without postulat-
ing a further basic category of entities. We will therefore speak
of the proposition that p as the referent of 'being such that p'
rather than of 'that p.'

We therefore say that *sentences* are true when and only when
the propositions that they can be used to express are true, and
sentences are false when and only when the propositions that
they can be used to express are false. In saying this, we presuppose the principle of the *primacy of the intentional,* a principle
that we defend in detail in Chapter 6.

We also say that to believe the proposition that p is to believe
that there is something that is such that p.

This statement would lead to contradiction if it were applied
to a person who believes the proposition that nothing exists.
The fault, however, does not lie in what I have been saying. It
lies in the assumption that there *can* be someone who believes
the proposition that nothing exists.

Aristotle pointed out that *man* and *existent man* are the same
thing (*Metaphysics*, Book IV, Ch. 2, 1004b). This fact is what led
Kant to say that "existence is not a predicate."[2]

I would agree with Kant that existence is not a predicate. If
you say, "I have 100 thalers," then you would not be adding
anything to what you've said if you went on to say, "And
what's more, they are 100 *existent* thalers." The sentences "I
believe that something exists" and "I believe that nothing ex-

24

ists," if taken literally, would have no content. What they express would not imply, with respect to any attribute, either that that attribute is exemplified or that it is not exemplified.

FACTS AND PROPOSITIONS

Facts may be reduced to propositions in the present sense of the term *proposition*. We may say, as others have done:

> D4   A *fact* is a true proposition

We gain some insight into this definition of fact by noting that *facts* and *true propositions* satisfy the identity criteria that we have formulated for attributes. The following is an application of these criteria to facts and true propositions.

> C1   *The fact that p* is identical to *the true proposition that p* if and only if *the fact that p* is necessarily such that anyone who has it as the content of an act of thinking has *the true proposition that p* as the content of an act of thinking, and conversely

PROPOSITIONS AND POSSIBLE WORLDS

If we need to speak of such things as *possible worlds*, then we may identify such entities with a certain type of proposition.

> D5   w is a *world* =Df w is a proposition such that for every proposition e, either w logically implies e or w logically implies the negation of e; and there is no proposition h such that w implies both h and the negation of h

(Here "w," "h," and "e" are used as terms; we avoid "p," "q," and "r," since we have not been using these letters as terms.)

A world is a self-consistent, maximal proposition. That it is maximal is guaranteed by the first clause of the definition, and that it is self-consistent is guaranteed by the second. Given the present system of concepts, there would seem to be no need to introduce any other sense of "possible world."

If possible worlds are thus reducible to propositions, and if propositions are reducible to attributes, then possible worlds are reducible to attributes.

THE SINGULAR-PROPOSITION VIEW

I remarked, at the beginning of this book, that it is not my primary concern to criticize the views of other philosophers. There is one view, however, that should be mentioned, for it is inconsistent with the present view and it seems to have been accepted by most philosophers who have attempted to state clearly how they interpret their use of the term *proposition*. This is the view that is sometimes called the *singular-proposition view*. According to this view, a that-clause of the form 'that N is F,' where 'N' is a proper name, refers to a proposition that literally contains the referent of 'N'.

The somewhat strange character of this view is best seen if we consider its application to certain propositions ostensibly about "nonexistent entities."

This view seems to have the consequence that if a person believes that Pegasus is a horse, then there exists a certain proposition that the person accepts, and this proposition has, as a constituent, an object that does not exist. Since such an entity is a whole made up of constituents some of which do not exist, it is quite unlike any whole that we have previously encountered. What good reason could there be for accepting such a view?[3] Our point is that there is no good reason for accepting an ontology that commits us to the existence of wholes that include nonexistent individuals among their constituents.

The defender of the singular proposition view might maintain that if a name 'N' does not refer to any existent entity, then it does not refer at all, and so there is no proposition re-ferred to by that-clauses involving 'N.' However, this response seems to have the implausible consequence that no one can believe that Pegasus is a horse.

The account of propositions that has been presented here avoids these problems.

5

THE INTENTIONAL STRUCTURE
OF ATTRIBUTES

INTRODUCTION

Some attributes are compounds of two or more other attributes. Of attributes that are compound, some are conjunctive and others are disjunctive. And compound as well as non-compound attributes may be either negative or positive.

In making these distinctions, we are not concerned primarily with language. We are concerned, rather, with the structure of those thoughts that we may use our language to express.

The distinctions that we make here presuppose the concept of intentional *content* that has already been introduced:

> D1 x has being-F as the content of an act of
> believing =Df x believes that something
> is F

We assume, as Descartes had done, that believing, or judging, presupposes thinking about:

> A1 The attribute of believing that there is F
> is necessarily such that whatever has it
> thinks about something being F

The term *believing* in this formula may be replaced by terms for other intentional acts.

NEGATIVE ATTRIBUTES AS CATEGORIALLY OPEN

We may keep some philosophical perspective by considering what Aristotle says about negation in *De Interpretatione*. He is discussing language and asks us to consider the expressions "does not recover" and "is not sick." He proposes to call these expressions *indefinite verbs* because, he says, they "hold indifferently of anything, whether existent or nonexistent."[1]

He is telling us that some attributes – for example, being non-red – are possibly such that they are exemplified by everything. Such attributes, therefore, are capable of being exemplified in every category. Hence we could call these attributes "categorially open." Other attributes – for example, being red – cannot be exemplified in every category. Such attributes may be called "categorially closed."

Aristotle tells us, then, that categorially open attributes, such as being non-red, may "hold indifferently of anything, whether existent or nonexistent." Thomas Aquinas, in commenting on this passage, points out that "nonexistent" is not here intended "with the force of privation," for "privation supposes a determinate subject." Rather, "nonexistent" is taken with the force of simple negation.[2] Neither Aristotle nor St. Thomas is here expressing the Meinongian view according to which nonexistent entities may be said to have certain properties.

The point may be put somewhat informally as follows. If we say that "A so and so is not a such and such," then we are attributing a privation to something; we are saying, in effect, that there *is* something that does *not* have the property of being a such and such. But if we say only that "It is not true that a so and so is a such and such," we are not attributing a privation to anything; we are saying merely that it is *not* true that there *are* any so and sos that *are* such and such.

The distinction that Aquinas here attributes to Aristotle is like the distinction that Bertrand Russell was to make between "the primary and the secondary occurrences of definite descriptions."[3] The descriptive phrase "the golden mountain" has a primary occurrence in "The golden mountain exists" and a secondary occurrence in "The golden mountain does not exist." The truth of the second statement (in which the occurrence is secondary), unlike the truth of the first, would not warrant the inference to "There *is* one and only one golden mountain."

Aristotle's remarks will help us to understand what we have been calling the intentional structure of attributes.[4]

COMPOUND ATTRIBUTES

It would be misleading to say that all compound attributes are compounds of attributes that are not compound. A conjunctive attribute, for example, may be a compound of attributes that are disjunctions; a disjunction may be a compound of attributes some of which are negations and others of which are conjunctions. Indeed, the possibilities may be multiplied ad indefinitum. But if there are compound attributes, then there are also noncompound attributes.

There are alternative ways of defining these compounds, just as there are alternative ways of defining the corresponding propositional concepts. We will present just one possibility.

NEGATIVE ATTRIBUTES

We first specify the sense in which being non-red and being red may be said to be *contingent* attributes. Then we specify the sense in which being non-red is *negative*.

> D2   P is a contingent attribute =Df P is an attribute that is possibly such that something exemplifies it and possibly such that nothing exemplifies it

Further complications are needed to formulate a definition of the more general concept of a *negative attribute*. Certain arbitrary decisions must be made in connection with mathematical attributes such as being finite and being infinite. But what we shall say is adequate for the purposes of the theory of categories.

There is an ambiguity in the expression "the negation of an attribute." We may interpret it broadly, with the result that (1) being non-red may be said to be the negation of being red and (2) being-red may be said to be the negation of being non-red. Or we may interpret it more narrowly, taking "is the negation of" to be asymmetrical: Being non-red is the negation of being red, so being red is not the negation of being non-red. We will take "is the negation of" in the asymmetrical sense.

We now formulate our definition of the concept of the negation of an attribute.

> D3   The attribute N is the negation of the attribute P =Df P and N are necessarily such that (1) nothing can have or lack both at once; (2) whoever can have N as the content of an act of believing can have P as the content of an act of believing; and (3) N is possibly such that it is exemplified by everything

The asymmetry of the relation "is the negation of" is guaranteed by the final clause of D3. If N is the negation of P, then P is not possibly such that it is exemplified by everything. Note also our account rules out the possibility that an attribute has two or more negations.

A *negative* attribute is an attribute that is the negation of an attribute; a *positive* attribute is an attribute that is not a negative attribute.

DISJUNCTIVE AND CONJUNCTIVE ATTRIBUTES

Our account of disjunctive and conjunctive attributes makes use of our intentional definition of conceptual entailment:

> D4   The attribute P conceptually entails the attribute Q =Df P is an attribute that is nec-

essarily such that whoever has it as the content of an act of believing has Q as the content of an act of believing

D5   The attribute D is a disjunction of attributes P and Q =Df (1) D is necessarily such that for all x, x exemplifies D if and only if either x exemplifies P or x exemplifies Q; (2) P does not conceptually entail D; (3) Q does not conceptually entail D; and (4) D conceptually entails both P and Q

D6   The attribute C is a conjunction of the attributes P and Q =Df (1) C is necessarily such that for all x, x exemplifies C if and only if x exemplifies P and x exemplifies Q; (2) P does not conceptually entail C; (3) Q does not conceptually entail C; and (4) C conceptually entails both P and Q

In the chapter that follows, we discuss the intentional point of view using the theory of attributes we have developed. In Chapters 7 and 8, we then discuss the categorial implications of *classes*, or *sets*, and of *relations*. But in Chapter 9, we discuss difficult questions that others have touched on only indirectly.

6

THE PRIMACY OF
THE INTENTIONAL

INTRODUCTION

By reflecting on the nature of ourselves, we can best understand the ultimate categories of reality – substances, states, and attributes. We now consider this intentional point of view in detail. In this way, we can best understand the present theory of categories.

We will begin with the problem of objective reference. What is it to have a thought that refers to something other than oneself? Is it our language that enables our thoughts to refer or is it our thoughts that enable our language to refer? We here defend the intentional point of view: It is our thoughts that enable our language to refer.

We will be led, finally, to formulate a *logical mark* of intentionality.

THE PROBLEM OF OBJECTIVE REFERENCE

It has often been said that the problem of objective reference is that of showing "how the mind gets out of the circle of its own ideas." If we can show how the mind – or, better, the person – may be said to have a belief that is directed on *a thing other than itself* and *only* on *that thing*, then we can solve the problem of objective reference. This is what we attempt to do.

Making use of our realist view of properties, we can give a relatively simple account of *de re* believing – an account of what it is for something x to be *believed by* someone S to have a certain property.[1]

Our account of properties provides us with the means of simplifying the problem. Instead of asking, *with respect to x,* what it is for it to have the property of being-F, we will ask, *with respect to the property of being-F,* what it is for it to be exemplified by x.

Our account will also enable us to deal with Wittgenstein's challenging question: "What makes my belief about you a belief about *you?*"[2]

There are two difficult questions that an account of *de re* believing must enable us to deal with. Both may be illustrated by reference to Robert Louis Stevenson's story *Dr. Jekyll and Mr. Hyde.* Most patients think that Dr. Jekyll is one person and Mr. Hyde another. But despite this mistake, Dr. Jekyll may still be said to be *believed by* most of his patients to be a physician. How can this be?

A related question may be illustrated by slightly complicating the story. We will suppose that, unknown to his patients and to most of the people in the community, Dr. Jekyll has a twin brother who looks just like him. A patient sees the brother and takes him to be Dr. Jekyll. Again, despite the mistake, Dr. Jekyll is believed by the patient to be a physician. How can this be if the patient has mistaken another person for Dr. Jekyll?

We may answer the question if we add an *epistemic* component to our account of *de re* believing. We make use, therefore, of our epistemic concept, expressed by "Believing that is more reasonable for S than believing that

> D1   S believes with respect to the property of being F that only x has it =Df (1) x is the only thing that is F; and (2) S believes that only one thing is F
>
> D2   S has a *de re* belief about x =df Either (1) x = S and there is a property P such that

36

S believes that he himself has P, or (2)
There is a property P such that:
  (i) x is the only thing that has P, and S
      believes with respect to P that only x
      has it
 (ii) if S also believes, with respect to some
      property Q other than P, that only x
      has Q, then S's belief with respect to P
      is more reasonable than S's belief with
      respect to Q, if Q is the negation of P,
      or at least as reasonable if Q is not the
      negation of P.

I here make use of Hector-Neri Castañeda's insight according
to which there is a distinction between what is expressed by
"S believes himself to have P" and "S believes S to have P."[3] (If
you are the suspect, you may believe that the suspect will be
arrested without believing that you yourself will be arrested.)

We have, then, an account of the way in which a person
"gets outside the circle of his own ideas." We also have answered Wittgenstein's question, "What makes my belief about
you a belief about *you?*"

Now we may turn to linguistic reference.

THE THEORY OF THE ENGLISH SAILOR

Consider the following observation by P. E. B. Jourdain:

Dr. Morgan said that, "if all mankind had spoken one language,
we cannot doubt that there would have been a powerful, perhaps universal school of philosophers who would have believed
in the inherent connexion between names and things; who
would have taken the sound *man* to be the mode of agitating
the air which is essentially communicative of the ideas of reason, cookery, bipedality, etc. . . . 'The French,' said the sailor,
'call a cabbage a *shoe;* the fools! Why can't they call it a cabbage,
when they must know it is one?' "[4]

The absolute view of language – or, better, the view of the
English sailor – is the view according to which there is an abso-

lute and eternal connection between words and the things they designate. But this view seems somewhat provincial.

What we should say is not simply that the sound "shoo" designates cabbages, but rather that some people use the sound "shoo" to designate cabbages, that some people use it to designate shoes, that some people use it to drive away unwanted animals, and so on.

We happen to use certain sounds or marks to express certain things. And in so doing, we mean to convey certain things.

What is meant, then, by "meaning to convey"? H. P. Grice has suggested that, in one of its senses, the locution 'A meant something by x' is "roughly equivalent to 'A intended the utterance of x to produce some effect in an audience by means of the recognition of this intention.'"[5] Here I present one way of carrying out this program. Hence I shall propose an intentional analysis of *meaning to convey.*

ADDRESSING AN UTTERANCE TO CONVEY SOMETHING

Suppose that you are driving a car in which I am a passenger and I say to you urgently: "That green Chevrolet over there is out of control!" If you reply "That's not a Chevrolet" you may correct what I say, but the part that you correct is not the part that I was concerned to convey. I might reply, if there is time, "Whatever make of car it is, it's out of control!"[6] The words "that green Chevrolet over there" in my original utterance need not have expressed any part of the *content* I meant to convey. It may be that I used them only so that you would pick out the *object* I want to convey something about. The *content* of my message was expressed by the words "out of control."

If I want to convey something to you, then I want to cause you to have a certain thought. But conveying a belief involves more than merely causing someone to believe something. Kant cites the following case of intended deception that is not a case of meaning to convey and therefore not a case of lying.

"I may wish people to think that I am off on a journey, and so I pack my luggage; people draw the conclusion I want them to draw. . . . I have not lied to them, for I have not stated that I am expressing my opinion."[7]

Kant's remark should not be taken to mean that in order to be able to tell you anything, I must first tell you that I am going to tell you something, and that in order to be able to convey anything, I must first convey that I'm going to convey something. This type of regress would hardly be acceptable.

The activity of meaning to convey involves both *intentional* concepts and *causal* concepts.

To address the problem Kant raises, we must make a distinction between *intending to cause* a person to believe something and *addressing* that thought to the person. We may put the distinction somewhat loosely by saying that if I *address* a thought to you, then I am intending not only to convey that thought but also to convey that *I am intending to convey* that thought.

The concept of *addressing an utterance* may now be defined as follows:

> D3   S addresses an utterance to z to convey
> the belief to z that y is F =Df S makes an
> utterance so that z will believe that S does
> this so that z will believe that y is F

In case the definiens gives the reader pause, it should be noted that the expression "so that z will believe" occurs twice. This is the way we deal with the Kantian problem previously described.

THE MEANING OF LINGUISTIC UTTERANCES

Suppose that I say to you, pointing: "That thing belongs to me." It would be a mistake to suppose that the demonstrative expression has the same sense for me that it has for you. We could thus speak of the "speaker's sense" and of the "hearer's

39

sense" of a demonstrative expression. The two senses vary with the conditions under which the expression is used.[8]

There is, then, an obvious analogy between the speaker's sense and the hearer's sense of the term that is being used. Possibly the speaker's sense of that term may be expressed by "the thing that I am pointing to," and the hearer's sense may be expressed by "the thing that is being pointed out to me." But we do not need to use demonstratives this way to explicate the sense of demonstratives.[9]

We may put the matter this way:

> D4   x uses W to designate y =Df x makes an utterance to bring it about that (1) W is perceived and that (2) this perception will result in y's becoming an object of thought[10]

An example would be the case of there being no devil and there being a person who believes himself to be persecuted by the devil. Suppose that the person uses "Satan" as a name for the devil. We cannot say, in this case, that he uses "Satan" to *designate* the devil. Let us say that in this case the person *means* to use "Satan" to designate the devil. The relevant concept is to be explicated this way:

> D5   x uses W with the attributive sense A =Df (1) x addresses an utterance in which W is used to designate y; and (2) A is the content of the belief that x intends to convey

According to our definition of the content of an act of believing, in Chapter 2, if you believe that there is F, then the property of being F is the content of your act of believing.[11]

In this way, then, I would defend the thesis of the primacy of the intentional. To evaluate such an analysis, we should also have before us competing analyses purporting to reduce intentional concepts to semantic concepts.[12]

A LOGICAL MARK OF THE INTENTIONAL

A *sentential prefix* is a phrase that, when added to the beginning of a sentence, yields a longer sentence. Such a prefix may be as long as one likes. An example is "If the weather is good and if Dion is feeling well, then." This is a prefix that, when added to "Dion is feeling well," will yield a sentence.

The definition and resulting thesis may be put this way:

> D6   C is a contingency-making prefix =Df C is a phrase that, when prefixed to a sentence, either necessary or contingent, yields a sentence that is contingent

> A1   Any sentence that begins with a contingency-making prefix is intentional

None of the usual modal operators (e.g., "it is possible that," "it is necessary that") is thus contingency-making. But such intentional prefixes as "John believes that" and "John wonders whether" are contingency-making. The result of prefixing any of them to any sentence at all, whether contingent or necessary, is contingent.

We have, then, a logical mark of the intentional.

PART TWO

The Basic Categories

7

THE ONTOLOGY OF THE THEORY
OF CLASSES

INTRODUCTION

Here we are concerned with the theory of classes, or set theory, but only to the extent that it is directly relevant to the theory of categories. This relevance is twofold. Boolean algebra, which is part of set theory, has been used by Frege and by Whitehead and Russell to make clear what *numbers* are. It has also been used by Kuratowski to make clear what *relations* are.

In this chapter, we consider how the subject matter of Boolean algebra may be reduced to attributes. In the following chapter, we consider how relations may be reduced to attributes.

CLASSES AND AGGREGATES

The terms *class* and *set* are used to refer to the subject matter of Boolean algebra. Sometimes they are used to refer to aggregates, heaps, or collections. Thus, since the concept of an aggregate, heap, or collection is relatively easy to grasp, it is concluded, mistakenly, that the Boolean sense of these terms is also relatively easy to grasp.

We can readily understand what it is, say, for there to be a collection of three dogs in a kennel. But the class of three dogs is not to be identified with the corresponding collection, even though the class has the three dogs as its members and the collection has these three dogs as its parts or constituents. We may say that the collection *corresponds* to the class, meaning only that the collection is the aggregate of the members of the class. But the collection of dogs in the kennel also corresponds to indefinitely many other classes. One such class is that of large-scale dog parts in the kennel (say, 3 heads, 3 torsos, 3 tails, and 12 feet), a class that has exactly 21 members. Another such class is the class of dog cells; still another is the collection of molecules that make up the dog cells.[1] The class of dogs has only dogs as members. But for every member that the class of dogs has, the class of dog parts has many members. Since each of the four classes (dogs, dog parts, dog cells, and dog molecules) corresponds to the one collection or heap of dogs, it would obviously be a mistake to identify the four classes with the one heap or collection.

And, a fortiori, it would be a mistake to identify a class of classes with the heap of corresponding heaps.

THE PROBLEM OF REDUCING CLASSES TO ATTRIBUTES

There is, of course, an obvious relation between attributes and classes. The class of rational animals, according to the traditional example, is the class of all and only those things that have the attribute of being a rational animal. But the identity conditions for classes are not the same as those for attributes.

The class of rational animals is identical to the class of featherless bipeds, for (let us assume that) all rational animals are featherless bipeds and all featherless bipeds are rational animals. But the *attribute* of being a rational animal is not the same as that of being a featherless biped. For the one attribute has attributes that the other does not. Thus, the attribute of being a rational animal, unlike that of being a featherless biped, is necessarily such that whatever has it is rational; and the attribute of being a featherless biped, unlike the attribute of being a rational animal, is necessarily such that whatever has it has feet.

Yet there would be an advantage to being able to reduce

classes or sets to attributes. For then we could preserve the truths of set theory without presupposing that, in addition to attributes, there are such entities as classes. And there would be other advantages to such a reduction.

According to Frege, and according to Whitehead and Russell, the propositions of arithmetic may be construed as propositions about that branch of the theory of classes, or set theory, that is Boolean algebra. And if they are right in thinking that they have shown this, then they may be said to have shown how those entities that we call numbers may be reduced to classes.

There is some disagreement among mathematicians about the question of whether numbers *are* reducible to sets or classes. But it is accurate to say, I think, that this disagreement does not turn on the question of whether Frege, Russell, and Whitehead succeeded in doing what they had set out to do. It turns, rather, on the philosophical question of whether what they succeeded in doing constitutes a reduction of arithmetic to set theory. Here we need say only that it constitutes a reduction in that sense of "reduction" that we have been using here.

Our present concern is ontology. Can sets or classes be reduced to attributes?

THE METHOD OF REDUCING CLASSES TO ATTRIBUTES

It is easy to translate *some* statements about classes into statements about attributes. Thus, to say "x is a member of the class of Fs" is to say that x exemplifies the attribute of being F. To say "the class of Fs includes the class of Gs" is to say that everything that is G is F. But we need a more general procedure.

If the axioms of set theory can be reformulated as true principles about attributes, then sets may be said to be reducible to attributes.

The following nine axioms are adequate for traditional set theory:[2]

(S1)   If A and B are classes, then there is the class, A + B, that is the *sum* of A and B – namely, the class of those things that are either members of A or members of B

(S2)   If A and B are classes, then there is the class A × B that is the *product* of A and B – namely, those things that are members of A and also members of B

(S3)   There is a class that is *the null class* – the class 0 that is such that, for every class A, A is identical to the sum of A and 0 (i.e., A + 0)

(S4)   There is a class that is *the universal class* – the class U that is such that, for every class A, A is identical to the product of A and U (i.e., A × U)

(S5)   If there is a universal class and a null class, then for every class A, there is the *negative* of A – the class -A that is such that (a) the sum of A and -A is identical to the universal class and (b) the product of A and -A is identical to the null class

(S6)   (A + B) is identical to (B + A)

(S7)   (A × B) is identical to (B × A)

(S8)   [A + (B × C)] is identical to [A + B) × (A + C)]

(S9)   [A × (B + C)] is identical to (A × B) + (A × C)].

Russell's reduction of classes to attributes

The principles of Boolean algebra may be reduced to principles about properties or attributes by following a procedure suggested by Russell and later modified by Carnap.[3]

Russell's original formula was essentially this:

"The class of x's such that x is F is so and so" may be replaced by "There is an attribute P, which is such that (1) P and being-F are exemplified by the same things and (2) P is so and so.

Carnap showed that the results would be more plausible if the existential quantifier were replaced by a universal quantifier.[4] In this case, the Russellian formula becomes:

"The class of x's such that x is F is so and so" may be replaced by "For every attribute P, if P and being -F are exemplified by the same things, then P is so and so."

To reduce the nine axioms to truths about attributes, three steps are sufficient: (1) replace *class* throughout by *attribute;* (2) replace *member* throughout by *instance;* and (3) replace *is identical to* throughout by *has the same instances as.*

The procedure is essentially this: Wherever a Boolean formula contains a locution of the form "The class of Fs is so and so," that locution is replaced by one of the form "For every attribute P, if P is exemplified by the same things as is the attribute of being F, then P is so and so."

What we know about sets or classes, then, does not require us to go beyond the list of categories that we have set forth.

8

THE NATURE OF RELATIONS

INTRODUCTION

Our concern in this chapter is to ensure that the theory of categories that we have defended is adequate to the nature of relations. Our concern is not with the logic of relations, but rather with the nature of those things that satisfy the formulas of the logic of relations. The views that we defend have been developed in their essentials by logicians of the present century. But relations throughout the history of Western philosophy have been entities of an extremely puzzling sort.

This puzzlement most naturally arises when one compares relations with attributes that are not relations. One then asks: How can there be such entities at all?

F. H. Bradley has provided a classic statement of this question:

> The relation is not the adjective of one term, for, if so, it does not relate. Nor for the same reason is it the adjective of each term taken apart, for then again there is no relation between them. Nor is the relation their common property, for then what keeps them apart? They are now not two terms at all, because not separate.[1]

We shall return to Bradley's problem after discussing the nature of the direction of relations.

ORDERED PAIRS

If John is fond of Mary, then the relation of being fond of is directed *from* John *to* Mary. It may also be that the relation is

51

not directed from Mary to John, for Mary may not be fond of John. To know what relations are, we must understand the concept of the *direction* of relations.

The concept of an *ordered pair* was introduced into set theory by Kasimierz Kuratowski.[2] He showed how to construe relations as those sets or classes that are ordered pairs. The concept is readily adapted to the theory of attributes.

Kuratowski identified the ordered pair "x paired with y" as the class whose only members are (1) the class whose only member is x and (2) the class whose only members are x and y. W. V. Quine provides this clear statement.

> *Dyadic* relations . . . relate elements in pairs. The relation of giving (y gives z to w) or betweenness (y is between z and w), on the other hand, is triadic; and the relation of paying (x pays y to z for w) is tetradic. But the theory of dyadic relations provides a convenient basis for the treatment also of such polyadic cases. A triadic relation among elements y, z and w, might be conceived as a dyadic relation born by y to z;w.[3]

There are many ways of distinguishing relations by reference to the number of terms that the relations may be said to have. Our concern is merely to find one that does not go beyond the present theory of categories and that is adequate to the concept of a relation. Oversimplifying somewhat, we may give one interpretation as follows:

> D1   R is an attribute that *orders* something x to something y =Df R is an attribute that has among its instances (1) an attribute that has x as its only instance and (2) an attribute that has x and y as its only instances

An example satisfying this formula would be the case in which Jones, who is the fastest runner, envies Smith, who is the fastest swimmer. (1) R is the relation of being envious of; (2) x is Jones; (3) y is Smith; (4) being the fastest runner is an attribute that only Jones has; (5) being the fastest swimmer is an attribute that only Smith has; and (6) being either the fastest runner or the fastest swimmer is a disjunctive attribute that only Jones and Smith have.

Application of the definition thus requires that each thing have an attribute that no other thing has. And, of course, if a thing has one such attribute, then it has many. (If the tallest man is wise, then only he has the attribute of being both the tallest and wise.)

> D2   A *one-term relation* is an attribute that does not possibly order anything

> D3   A *two-term relation* is an attribute that possibly orders a one-term relation to another one-term relation

Let us say that an attribute orders x and y, provided only that it orders either x *to* y or y *to* x.

> D4   A *three-term relation* is an attribute that possibly orders a one-term relation and a two-term relation

The next definition is one that, given the foregoing definitions, may be used in defining relations of any order.

> D5   An *n*-term relation is an attribute that possibly orders a one-term relation and an (*n* − one)-term relation

And so on.

DOES THE CONCEPT OF A RELATION INVOLVE A VICIOUS REGRESS?

What is a vicious regress? Or, better, what does it mean to be confronted by such a regress? One is confronted with a *vicious infinite regress* when one attempts a task of the following sort: Every step needed to begin the task requires a preliminary step. What Bradley seems to have thought about the nature of relations does illustrate what such a confrontation with an infinite regress would be.

One could say that no two things can be related unless there is a relation that ties them together. The relation of *tying* would confront us with a vicious regress if it were of this sort: (1) the only way to tie two things together is to connect them with a rope, and (2) the only way to connect two things with a rope is to use two more ropes – one of them to tie the first rope to the *first* thing and the other to tie that same rope to the *second* thing. In such a situation, we could never tie two things together; as Bradley might put it, "we would be forced to go on tying new ropes without end." And we would be unable ever to find out whether two things are tied together, for we could not learn whether any given rope is tied to anything until we found out whether there was another rope that tied the first rope to that thing.

But this is not the way tying works. One rope will do for tying two things together. There is no reason at all to suppose that relating confronts us with the kind of tying just considered. We need not conclude, therefore, that relations confront us with a vicious infinite regress.

These considerations are sufficient to show that since our theory of categories provides a place for attributes, it also provides a place for relations.

9

TIMES AND THE TEMPORAL

INTRODUCTION

It is commonly believed, at least among philosophers, that there are such entities as *times*, that our knowledge of these entities is what enables us to identify and individuate events, and that the concept of *a time* is essential to the concept of *an event*. But here I present a theory of events that does not presuppose that there are such things as times. It avoids the difficult questions that the assumption of such entities involves, and it enables us to develop a relatively simple ontology. We should be clear about what the statement does *not* tell us. It does not tell us that the event in question bears a relation to a type of entity that is neither a state nor an individual thing nor an abstract object. In short, it does not tell us that the event bears a certain relation to a time. I try to show in detail that such a theory enables us to deal with what would otherwise be extraordinarily difficult ontological puzzles. And it does not deprive us of anything we are likely to miss.

QUESTIONS ABOUT THE CONCEPT OF A TIME

The concept of a time involves two types of problem. One is epistemological, the other ontological.

The general epistemological question about times is: How do we find out anything about their nature? The current philosophical uses of the concept of a time require us to distinguish one time from another. How do we go about doing this?

The second question is ontological. Do times come into being or pass away? Consider what would be an earlier time – say that time that would have been 12 midnight, Rocky Mountain time, December 31, 1900. Does that time still exist? If it does still exist, then why can't we be said to exist at that time?

Or is there something more to existing *at* a time than *coexisting with* that time? If there is something more to existing at a time, what could it be? It would hardly do to say: "There are only certain higher-order times at which a thing is at any given lower-order time." But if the time we have been discussing *did exist* but *no longer* exists, what are we to say of that event that was the *ceasing to be* of the time? In trying to construct a theory of events, we would need a very good reason before committing ourselves to the existence of events of that kind.

The assumption that there *are* times, as I will try to show, multiplies entities beyond necessity.

PAST, PRESENT, AND FUTURE

Whether or not there are things that are times, there are temporal attributes of things, and things stand in temporal relations.

Using a language that, like our ordinary language, is tensed, one may say that whatever exists exists now. And since the language *is* tensed, the "now" in "Whatever exists exists now" is redundant and the statement is logically true. But there *were* things that no longer exist and there *will be* things that do not yet exist.

Some things have what may be called *temporally oriented properties.* Consider any repeatable property – say, moving. This is a property that is possibly such that there is something that *does not* have it but *did* have it and *will* have it. We may distinguish these nine possibilities:

(1) x is such as to be moving;
(2) x was such as to be moving;
(3) x will be such as to be moving;
(4) x is such as to have moved;
(5) x was such as to have moved;
(6) x will be such as to have moved;
(7) x is such as to be going to move;
(8) x was such as to be going to move;
(9) x will be such as to be going to move.

Our ordinary languages – not only ordinary English – have difficulty with the distinction between (2) and (4) and between (3) and (9). But it is easy to adjust our language to these distinctions. The proper procedure may be suggested by Arthur Prior's remark: Instead of saying "It will be the case that I eat my breakfast" we could say "It will be the case that I am eating my breakfast"; and instead of saying "I was eating my breakfast" we could say "It was the case that I am eating my breakfast."[1]

The attributes expressed in (2), (5), and (8) may be said to be past oriented and those expressed in (3), (6), and (9) to be future-oriented. The relevant concepts may be defined as follows:

D1   P is a repeatable attribute =Df P is possibly such that there exists an x such that x had P, x does not have P, and x will have P

D2   P is an attribute that is oriented toward the present =Df (1) P is an attribute that is necessarily such that whatever has it either did have or will have attributes; (2) P is possibly such that whatever has it had no attributes; and (3) P is possibly such that whatever has it will have no attributes

D3   P is an attribute that is oriented toward the past =Df (1) P is an attribute that is necessarily such that whatever has it had attributes; and (2) P is possibly such that whatever has it will have no attributes

D4   P is an attribute that is oriented toward the future =Df (1) P is an attribute that is necessarily such that whatever has it will have attributes; and (2) P is possibly such that whatever has it had no attributes

One may object: In supposing that there are such attributes as having moved and going to move, you are ignoring the fact that language may be tenseless. What is the force of this objection? Let us compare the following two sentences, U (for "untensed") and T (for "tensed"):

(U) There *are* dinosaurs.

Are is italicized to indicate that it is tenseless.

(T) There were dinosaurs or there are dinosaurs or there will be dinosaurs.

Is U logically equivalent to T?

If U is not logically equivalent to T, then either (1) what is expressed by U fails to imply what is expressed by T or (2) what is expressed by T fails to imply what is expressed by U. In the case of (1), we may well wonder what reason there is for thinking U to be true. In the case of (2), we may ask: What *more* does U tell us than T does? I have no idea how this question might be answered.

The mere fact that a sentence may be constructed without using any expressions in the past or future tenses would seem to have very little philosophical significance.

DO WE NEED TEMPORAL QUANTIFIERS?

Let us now ask about *temporal quantifiers.* If we deny that there are such individual things as times, we will also say, of course, that there never were and never will be such individual things as times. But there *were* individual things that no longer exist, and presumably there *will be* individual things that do not yet exist. Do we need past-tensed and future-tensed quantifiers to express these facts? In such a case, we would have three quantifiers:

There existed an x such that . . . x . . .

There exists an x such that . . . x . . .

There will exist an x such that . . . x . . .

We need only the present-tensed quantifier; the other two quantifiers may be explicated in terms of it.

The first dichotomy in our table of categories is a division of all things into (1) contingent beings and (2) necessary beings (*entia necessaria*). This division will be discussed in Chapter 10.

If there once was a philosopher who drank hemlock and who *no longer* exists, then there always will be something – for example, the attribute being blue – that *once was*, such that there *is* a philosopher who is drinking the hemlock. And since Socrates is one of those things that came into being, then the property blue once *was* such that there *will be* something that *is* drinking the hemlock.

We will say, then:

> D4   There existed an x such that x was F =Df
> There exists a y that was such that there
> exists an x such that x is F

> D5   There will exist an x that x will be F =Df
> There exists a y that will be such that there
> exists an x such that x is F

TEMPORAL RELATIONS

Do temporal relations involve the concept of a time?

States are what, in the first instance, constitute the terms of temporal relations; and events will be construed here as being a subcategory of states.

Given the concept of *wholly preceding*, it is easy to define the other temporal relations that may obtain among events. The following definitions, for example, were set forth by Russell in "Order in Time" (1936):[2]

> x and y overlap =Df x does not wholly precede y; and y does not wholly precede x
>
> x begins before y =Df There is a z such that (a) x and z overlap and (b) z wholly precedes y
>
> x ends after y =Df There is a z such that (a) x and z overlap and (b) y wholly precedes z
>
> x ends before y =Df There is a z such that (a) x wholly precedes z and (b) x and z overlap

These definitions, like the others that we have formulated, are given in the present tense and therefore define the present-oriented versions of the concepts concerned.

We begin by considering the relation of wholly preceding – a relation that the First World War bore to the Second. Russell has shown that by taking this relation as undefined, one may go on to define the other temporal relations.[3] His analyses may readily be adapted to the present approach. I will not spell out Russell's definitions of other temporal concepts. The logical properties of these concepts may be illustrated by reference to those events that were the rule of Stalin, the presidency of Franklin D. Roosevelt, and the Second World War. The presidency of Roosevelt overlapped with the Second World War; the rule of Stalin overlapped with something that wholly preceded the war and with something that the war wholly preceded; the presidency of Roosevelt overlapped with something that wholly preceded the war; and the war overlapped with something that the presidency of Roosevelt wholly preceded.

60

HOW MANY TIMES HAS x BEEN F?

We now make explicit three ontological presuppositions of the present theory of categories.

> A1   There exists an x and there exists a y that
> are such that y *was* such that x does not
> exist

It follows that there is something that has come into being. You and I may be plausible examples.

> A2   There exists an x that is necessarily such
> that there exists *no* y that is, was, or will
> be such that x does not exist

Hence there is something that will not pass away. *Entia necessaria*, such as the number 7 and the attribute of being blue are examples.

> A3   For every x, if x is an *ens necessarium*, then
> x has an attribute P that is necessarily such
> that for every y, y is such that something
> has P

According to our assumptions, the attribute of being blue is an *ens necessarium*. It follows from this assumption that everything has the attribute (P) of being such that there is something that is exemplified if and only if there is something that is blue.

Clearly, every attribute is of this nature. Thus, the attribute of being a round square is necessarily such that it is exemplified if and only if there is something that is both round and square. And this attribute, which we have attributed to the attribute of being a round square, is also an attribute of the attribute of being blue.

Our assumption, according to which there are things that have come into being, enables us to give a sense to such expressions as "the first time," "the second time," and "the *n*th time," and to do so without supposing that there are such entities as times.

Consider this situation. You are with someone who is seeing a zebra for the first time; you are seeing it, too, but unlike your companion, you have seen a zebra before. You saw one not yesterday but the day before yesterday, and you had never seen a zebra before that. Hence you have the following attribute P that your companion does not have: being such as to have been (P') *both* such that (1) you are *not seeing* a zebra and (2) you *had seen* a zebra. The attribute P is a past-oriented attribute that you have now; and the attribute P' is a conjunction of two attributes that you had yesterday, one of them past oriented. Your companion, who is seeing a zebra for the first time, does not have the past-oriented attribute P.

And so we will say:

> D6   x is F for the first time =Df (1) x is F; and
> (2) x is not such that it was both non-F
> and such that it had been F

The second clause of the definiens may be spelled out further as follows: x *is* not such that it *was* such that it *is* non-F and *was* F. (I remind the reader of what was said earlier about the problems our ordinary language has with the expression of temporally oriented properties.)

Our definition puts us in a position to add two more definitions:

> D7   x is F for at least the nth time =Df (1) x is
> F; and (2) x was both non-F and such that
> it had been F for the $(n - 1)$ time

> D8   x is F for not more than the nth time =Df
> (1) x is F; and (2) it is false that x was both
> non-F and such that it had been F for at
> least the nth time

To say what it is for x to be F for the *second* time, we replace "the $(n-1)$ time" in D8 by "the first time" and replace "the *n*th time" in D8 by "the second time." In so doing, we apply the following:

> D9 x is F for the *n*th time =Df (1) x is F for at least the *n*th time; and (2) x is F for not more than the *n*th time

The result tells us what it is for x to be F for the *third* time. We may continue this way, step by step. We are not introducing a complexity that the subject matter does not have. This is how we would have to proceed if we want to define expressions containing *dates* – expressions of the form "x is F at *n*," where *n* might be replaced by "12 midnight, GMT, December 31, 1999."

The four definitions just given (D6 to D9) are readily put into the past and future tenses. Thus, the past-tense version of D6 would be:

> x was such that it is F for the first time = Df x was such that (1) it is F and (2) it is not such that it was both non-F and such that it had been F

We may say, then, that a thing has had a given attribute a certain number of times. We do not thereby commit ourselves to saying that there *are* times when an event has occurred. Nor do we commit ourselves to the thesis that events are the things that *recur*. In the following chapter, we make it clear that there are no events that do not occur. It follows from this that to say of an event that it occurs is to say that it exists. But nothing can have more than one beginning of existence. And therefore, no event may be said to recur.

Doesn't *anything* recur? In the following chapter, we also describe the sense in which attributes may be said to be the things that recur.

ATTRIBUTES THAT ARE TEMPORALLY ORIENTED

We have assumed that there are temporally oriented attributes. Thus, there are attributes that point toward the future (e.g., being such that it is going to walk) and there are attributes that point toward the past (e.g., being such that it did walk). Every attribute that is exemplified points toward the present.

It should be noted that only beginnings and endings are without duration. Other events, such as walking or sitting, are necessarily such that they have duration.

INTERPRETING EXPRESSIONS THAT ARE DATES

To be able to explicate expressions that are dates, we must understand what a *calendar* is. The following definition is taken from the *Encyclopaedia Britannica:* "A calendar is a device for reckoning time by regular divisions, or periods, and using them to date events."[4]

How are we to interpret the date that appears in such statements as "Such and such an event occurred on January 1, 1900"? Roughly speaking, we may say that, according to the usual interpretation, such a statement tells us that the event in question occurred 1,900 years after the event that was the birth of Jesus Christ. More generally, for some unit length t of time measurement, such a sentence tells us that the event occurred so many ts after a certain other event.

An analogous account may be given about the function of *clocks* and about the interpretation of such statements as "The time at which the event occurred was 5:15." The philosophical questions that concern us may be formulated by reference to such private clocks as stopwatches. "The time taken by the winner was just three minutes" might be taken to mean: "Between the event that was the signal for the start of the race and the event that was the winner crossing the finish line, there were 180 rotations of the hand of the watch."

Our philosophical question concerns the meaning of terms that are used as *dates*. And as far as that question is concerned, it would be sufficient to consider those calendars that might be kept by people who are out of touch with civilization – for example, people lost at sea or taken hostage. "This is day 2,745" might be used to mean "There have been 2,744 days (or revolutions of the Earth) since the event that was my arrival here." (One may also say: "There have been 2,744 days since the time of my arrival here." But this would add nothing since it only repeats the concept that we want to analyze.)

A MEAN BETWEEN EXTREMES

The question about *illusion* with which we are here concerned has been formulated in very different ways. These include not only "Is the passage of time an illusion?" but also "Is time unreal?", "Is becoming a mere subjective phenomenon?", and "Is our use of tense deceptive?"

There have been many attempts to prove that the passage of time *is* illusory, but I shall consider only three of them: (I) the Kantian considerations that influenced many of the idealistic philosophers of the nineteenth century; (II) the celebrated attempt by McTaggart to prove that the concepts of past, present, and future are inherently contradictory; and (III) the attempt by subsequent philosophers of science to prove not that these concepts are contradictory, but that they are simply illusions of the human mind.

(I) A simplified version of the Kantian type of proof can be found in Schopenhauer's *Essays*, which states: "He who is aware that the present moment has its source in us, and springs, that is, from within and not from without, cannot doubt of the indestructability of his own nature."[5] The argument takes as its premise the thesis that the present moment "has its source" in us and "springs from within." Schopenhauer then reasons this way:

(1) We are so constituted that we cannot be aware of anything without being aware of it *as being in the present moment.*

Therefore:

(2) *Without* our awareness, nothing could thus be said to be in the present moment.

Obviously, the conclusion does not follow from the premise. And we look in vain for another plausible premise that would satisfactorily complete the derivation.

The situation is similar when we turn to Kant himself. Kant affirms (1) early in the "Transcendental Aesthetic":

(1) Time is a necessary representation that underlies all intuitions. . . . In it alone is actuality of appearances possible at all.[6]

This thesis is quite plausible, especially if it is taken to imply that our experience always involves the experience of something *temporal.* But Kant then goes on to affirm (2):

(2) Time is *nothing but* the form of inner sense, that is, of the intuition of ourselves and of our inner state.[7]

The derivation turns, of course, on "nothing but."

We have here the familiar fallacy that has been associated with nineteenth-century idealism: the fallacy of identifying a *ratio cognoscendi* with a *ratio essendi.*

Do we find in the Kantian argument a good reason for believing that the passage of time is illusory? Our question does not concern the place of this thesis in Kant's system of philosophy. We are asking, more simply, whether there is anything there that will help *us* in *our* inquiry. The answer seems clearly negative.

(II) We turn next to one of the most celebrated attempts to prove that the passage of time is illusory: the proof formulated by McTaggart in Volume Two of *The Nature of Existence*. McTaggart tries to prove that "time is unreal."[8] In so doing, he attempts to show that such concepts as *past, present,* and *future* do not apply to anything.

McTaggart distinguishes two types of ostensible temporal relation – the A-series and the B-series. The A-series are those temporal relations that essentially involve the notions of past, present, and future. The B-series, on the other hand, are those temporal relations that can be characterized in terms of earlier and later. McTaggart attempts to show that the A-series involves a contradiction. The argument may be stated as follows:

(1) "Past, present, and future are incompatible determinations. Every event must be one or the other, but no event can be more than one. . . . The characteristics are therefore incompatible."

(2) If any event has one of them, then it has them all. "If *M* is past, it has been present and future. If it is future, it will be present and past. If it is present, it has been future and will be past.

Therefore:

(3) No event is past, present, or future.

Surely there is no ground for affirming (2). McTaggart himself sees that there is a difficulty, and he attempts to deal with it. We may put what he says in the form of a second argument:

(1′) It is never true . . . that M *is* present, past, and future. It *is* present, *will be* past, and *has been* future. Or it *is* past, and *has been* future and present, or again *is* future, and *will be* present and past. The characteristics are only incompatible when they are simultaneous, and there is no contradiction to this in the fact that each term has them all successively.

(2') When we say that X *has been* Y, we are asserting X *to be* Y at a moment of past time. When we say that X *will be* Y, we are asserting X *to be* Y at a moment of future time. When we say that X is Y (in the temporal sense of 'is'), we are asserting X *to be* Y at a moment of present time.[9]

Therefore:

(3') The A-series involves a contradiction.

But we have been given no ground for premise (2') of this argument. We have no reason for supposing that when one asserts X *to have been* Y, one is asserting X *to be* Y "at a moment of past time"; and we have no reason for supposing that when one says that X *will be* Y, one is asserting X *to be* Y "at a moment of future time." What reason do we have for supposing that if I say that you once *were* a child, I am saying that you *are* a child in the past? And what reason is there for supposing that if I see that you *will be* old, I am saying that you *are* old in the future?

Or could we put all of these premises in a tenseless language, thus avoiding the danger of confusing an "is" that is tensed with one that is untensed? In this case, our problem will be that of making the *first* premise plausible – the premise according to which past, present, and future may be said to be *incompatible* characteristics.

(III) We now consider the view according to which the *experience of time* and what is sometimes called the *experience of becoming* are illusions of the human mind and therefore false. Adolf Grünbaum provides an influential contemporary statement of this view. He says that the so-called transiency of time has "an inherent dependence on consciousness," and he takes this to imply that "the transiency of the Now is not also a feature of physical time."[10]

Attempts to prove that some generally accepted body of beliefs is false often appeal to premises that they are designed to discredit. This criticism can be applied to the doctrine usually attributed to Pyrrho, according to which *all* of our beliefs about the nature of things are unreasonable. To be sure, there *are* general beliefs that are false and also so widespread that perhaps they may be called errors of the human mind. Our beliefs about the motions of the Earth and of the heavenly bodies may provide one illustration. But these beliefs can hardly be called illusions, for they are systematically correctible. And our beliefs about the objects of immediate sensory experience are even more appropriate in the present context.

Consider those things that are variously called *sense impressions, sense data,* and *appearances,* and that are also referred to as *ways of sensing* and *ways of being appeared to.* Grünbaum writes:

> Common-sense color attributes, for example, surely *appear to be* properties of physical objects independently of our awareness of them and are held to be such by common sense. And yet scientific theory tells us that they are mind-dependent qualities the way that sweet and sour are.[11]

But just what is it that scientific theory is here being said to tell us? Since the days of the Greek skeptics, most epistemologists have agreed on the negative conclusion, according to which these sensory things do *not* have the status that we commonly believe them to have. But there has been no general agreement at all about the status that such things *do* have. Since our concern is to develop an adequate theory of categories, we cannot be content with the conclusion merely that there are certain sensory things that depend on minds.

It is reasonable to withhold commitment to this version of skepticism.

10

STATES AND EVENTS

INTRODUCTION

Since we have rejected the view that, in addition to properties and individual things, there are such entities as times, our theory of events is a theory of *events without times*. It replaces the undefined concept of *a time* with the undefined concept of *a state*. Hence we reject the view of Jaegwon Kim, according to which an event is "a structure consisting of a substance, a property and a time."[1]

Such an approach to events has the advantage of not requiring that only substances be the substrates of events. It also allows us to say that those states that consist of *one state contributing causally to another state* are also events. Such states, one could even say, are events par excellence. If one were asked to give a paradigmatic example of an event, one would, in all probability, cite an example of such an event.[2]

We begin, then, by formulating several principles about the nature of states.

THE NATURE OF STATES

Contingent things are here divided into those that are states and those that are not states. Contingent things that are not states are individuals. Contingent individuals, in turn, are divided into those that are ontologically dependent on other individuals and those that are not dependent on other individu-

71

als. Those that are thus dependent are *boundaries;* those that are not are *substances.*

Events are here construed as being a subcategory of states. The concept of a *state* is taken as undefined, but we may clarify it in several ways. In so doing, we will presuppose the extreme or Platonic realism already defended.

Suppose that you are reading. Then the following entities are involved: (1) the *contingent substance* that is yourself; (2) the *noncontingent thing* that is *the property of reading;* and (3) the contingent *state* that is *you reading.* It will be useful to say that you are the *substrate* of that state and that the property of reading is the *content.*

We first formulate a general principle about the existence of states.

> A1   For every x, x is F if and only if there is
>   the state x-being-F

The second principle tells us that every state is necessarily such that it has the substrate that it has.

> A2   For every x, the state x-being-F is neces-
>   sarily such that it is a state of x

And the third principle tells us that every state is necessarily such that it has the content that it has:

> A3   For every property P, if there is the state
>   x-having-P, then that state is necessarily
>   such that it is a state of having the prop-
>   erty P

Principle A3 would be trivial if the term *necessarily* were moved from its present place to a place immediately following the quantifier. "Necessarily all rational beings are rational," unlike "All rational beings are necessarily rational," does not tell us anything about the essential properties of rational beings.

From the fact that the *state* that is you reading something is necessarily such that it is a state of you, it does *not* follow, of course, that *you* are necessarily such that you are reading.

If there were no contingent individuals, then there would be indefinitely many nonessential properties that *everything* would have – for example, the property of being such that there are no dogs and the property of being such that there are no unicorns. Hence, even if there were no contingent individuals, there would be indefinitely many contingent states. According to some theologies, God would have the nonessential property of being such that there are *no* contingent things. In a similar way, God would have the property of being such that there *are* contingent things. Such nonessential properties are all-or-nothing properties; that is, they are necessarily such that either everything has them or nothing has them.

In what follows, I begin with some preliminary considerations that are relevant to the general problem of events.

I first consider certain distinctions Roman Ingarden has made. Then I turn to the theory of events that has been developed by Jaegwon Kim and is now associated with his name. Working from his theory, I develop an alternative.

Kim's theory and the one that I present here each presuppose that events cannot recur. It follows that causation may not be defined in terms of "constant conjunctions of events."

I turn, finally, to a positive account of *causation* and show how this concept may be analyzed within the ontology of the present theory of categories.

BEGINNINGS, ENDINGS, AND ENDURING STATES

In the twentieth century, one of the pioneering discussions of the ontological status of events is that of Roman Ingarden, who distinguishes beginnings, processes, and events.

Ingarden says, of what he calls *events*, that they have no duration. "They begin to be and thereupon cease to be. They are, so to speak, end-points or beginnings."[3] He gives us the following examples of events: "the collision of two bodies, the arrival of a train in a station, a light's being turned on, the death of a person."[4] Each of these examples is an instance of something that is *instantaneous*.

Ingarden concedes that he uses the term *event* much more narrowly than it is ordinarily used. (See Vol. I, p. 193.) And it is certainly true that the English word *event* is used much more broadly than Ingarden uses the German equivalent – *Ereignis*. But we cannot confidently say that he is *misusing* the term. The Polish general Jarulzelski was once quoted, in translation, as saying: "Reconciliation is a process, not an event."

Our use of *event* differs from that of Ingarden. We agree with him in saying that those states that are *beginnings* "exist only for an instant." We also agree that those states that are *processes* endure and therefore "exist for more than an instant."

The following concepts are essential to the account that we give:

> D1   x is a *beginning* =Df (1) x is a state, and (2)
> there is nothing that x did exemplify

> D2   x is an *ending* =Df (1) x is a state, and (2)
> there is nothing that x will exemplify

We should recall John Locke's dictum: "Nothing has two beginnings of existence." This dictum is entirely consistent with the statement that a state may *include* a multiplicity of beginnings and endings of *states*.

> D3   x is *coming into being* =Df x is such that
> there are no attributes that it had

This is enough to guarantee that coming into being is instantaneous. It is also enough to guarantee that a thing x, when it is coming into being, is such that it had not previously come into being. For if it had come into being previously, then there *would* be properties that it formerly had.

D4   x is *ceasing to be* (x is *passing away*) =Df x is
     such that there are no properties that it
     will have

This definition implies that x will not come into being again.

If we wish our theory to be adequate to the fact that Socrates, Plato, and Aristotle, even if they no longer exist, still have the attribute of *being admired,* then we may modify the preceding account. We may say that if a thing x is passing away, then there are no *internal attributes* that x is going to have. The needed concept is this:

D5   P is an attribute that is *internal to sub-
     stances* =Df P is necessarily such that (1)
     only substances can have it and (2) if it
     implies an attribute Q that substances can
     have, then whatever has P has Q

(Here "P implies Q" may be taken to abbreviate "P is necessarily such that if it is exemplified, then Q is exemplified." Note that P may imply Q even if some things that have P do not have Q.)

Being admired is thus an attribute that is not internal. For being admired implies being an admirer, and some things that are admired are not admirers.

These considerations enable us to single out two concepts that are essential to the theory of events.

First, where Ingarden uses *process,* I use *enduring state.*

D6   x is an *instantaneous* state =Df x is both a
     beginning and an ending

D7   x is an enduring state =df x is not an in-
     stantaneous state

An enduring state of a contingent thing is a state that is a *temporal* whole – a whole having as parts states that have incompatible contents and that are related by *before* and *after.* Such a whole, therefore, involves *change.* We explain (proper) parthood of states as follows:

75

D8   The content of state x is part of the content of state y =df The content of y implies
the content of x; and the content of x does
not imply the content of y

D9   State x is part of state y =df Either (1) the
substrate of x is a proper part of the substrate of y or (2) the content of x is part of
the content of y

If *me being seated* is an enduring state, then because I am a
changing thing, there is a present state *me being seated and F*
and a past state *me being seated and non-F.* Both of these states
are parts of *me being seated.* (We can replace this talk of "present" and "past" states with talk of states whose contents are
"oriented toward the present" and "oriented toward the past,"
as we saw in Chapter 9.)

One's entire life is a single enduring state – one that could
be called one's *history* or *biography.* And, more generally, everything is such that either it is going through its history or it is
beginning its history. Hence we may speak of the various *stages*
and *limits* of the history of a thing – or, to use more technical
terms, of the *temporal parts* and *slices* of that history. But we
must not make the category mistake of supposing that such
temporal parts and slices of a thing's history are also parts and
slices of the thing that *has* the history. *Space-time* is that enduring state that has as its substrate the sum or *collectivum* of all
the contingent individuals that there will have been.

HIGHER-ORDER STATES AND THE CONCEPT OF AN EVENT

We have assumed the following principle: For every x, there is
the state x-being-F if and only if x is F. Our assumptions imply,
therefore, that there are infinitely many states. They also imply that each state is a member of an infinite hierarchy of
states. The hierarchy may be illustrated this way:

(1) x-being-F;

(2) (x-being-F)-being-G;

(3) [(x-being-F)-being-G]-being-H.

An instance of (1) would be Jones walking. An instance of (2) would be (Jones walking) being strenuous. And an instance of (3) would be (Jones walking being strenuous) contributing causally to (Jones being tired).

We could say that a *first-order* state is a state of a substance. A *second-order* state is a state of a first-order state. An example of a first-order state is a state that is one first-order state contributing causally to another first-order state.

To say what an event is, we refer to the concepts of a first-order state and a second-order state:

> D10   x is a *first-order state* =Df x is a state of a
>   substance

> D11   x is a *second-order state* =Df x is a state of a
>   first-order state

We are now in a position to characterize the concept of an event.

> D12   x being F is an *event* =Df (1) x-being-F is
>   either a first-order state or a second-order
>   state; and (2) x is not necessarily such that
>   it is F

The second clause ("x is not necessarily such that it is F") presupposes that we wish to exclude from the class of events such nonhappenings as Jones's uncle being either tall or not tall.

In some of his writings on the concept of an event, Kim suggests a theory according to which all events are first-order states.[5] Such a restriction provides no place for those paradigmatic events that consist of one event *contributing causally* to the occurrence of another event. Examples are the striking of a match contributing causally to the burning of a piece of paper, the treatment of a patient contributing causally to the patient's being cured, and the rush of the sea contributing causally to the destruction of the pier. Here we have second-order events that relate first-order events.

If we want to do justice to the ordinary use of *event*, then we will restrict its use to states of lower order. We should require first-order states and second-order states to be called *events*, but since we must draw the line somewhere, we will not refer to states of higher order as events.

A CRITERION OF IDENTITY FOR EVENTS

Even though we do not define the concept of a state, we should be able to formulate a *criterion of identity* for states and therefore also for events. Such a criterion would tell us the conditions under which a state x may be said to be *identical to* a state y.[6]

Our criterion of state identity, and therefore also of event identity, is this:

> C1   x-being-F is the same state as y-being-G if
> and only if x is identical to y and being-F
> is identical to being-G

RECURRENCE: ETERNAL AND OTHERWISE

Any entity that undergoes change is the substrate of an *enduring state*. Since we say "*any* entity," our assertion is not restricted to those lower-order states that constitute events. Therefore, not all enduring states are events. Events, we have said, are either first-order or second-order states. But beginnings, endings, enduring states, and events are all states. As states, they are one-time things; they do not recur.

Some have held, however, that there are two kinds of events: (1) the one-time things that we have been discussing and that do not recur and (2) generic events that *do* recur.

What reason do we have for thinking that there are such generic events?

If we were to say that there are such generic events, then, once again, we would be multiplying entities beyond necessity. The facts that seem to require the addition of recurrable events to our ontology may be so construed that they require only the existence of nonrecurrable events.

Suppose that I was standing, then sitting, and then standing again. The criterion of event identity that we have formulated does not allow us to say that, in such a case, my standing recurs. Yet it is doubtless convenient to speak of recurrence in this context. And we may speak, if we choose, of the recurrence of the attribute of standing. I propose, then, the following definition, which allows us to attribute recurrence to *attributes* instead of to *events*.

> D13   The attribute of being-F recurs in the case
> of x =Df (1) x is F; and (2) x has been
> such that it ceased to be F

We may also state the definiens by saying: "x has been such that it was F for the first time." And so we may *have recurrence* and yet say that *no event recurs.*

Nietzsche suggested a kind of statistical argument to show that the history of the world has already repeated itself an infinite number of times and that it will repeat itself an infinite number of times.[7] The thought of such recurrence, according to Nietzsche, is "the most oppressive of all thoughts"; it is a "disciplinary thought" that "brings about the strength of superman" (p. 425). The troubling thing about such a thought, he said, is *not* the consequence that we have been through it all before and will go through it all again – and again and again. It is rather the thought of "the very aimlessness" of such a world.

But what of the thought that may be more disturbing to those of us who have lesser natures – the thought that we *have* been through it all before and will do so again? Whether or not the doctrine of eternal recurrence is true, unless there is reason to believe that *we ourselves* are eternal objects, there is no good reason to believe that we have been through it all more than once. As we have said, it follows from the nature of coming into being and passing away that nothing can have these attributes a second time. And we have found no good reason for supposing that we have existed throughout eternity.[8]

THE CONCEPT OF CAUSATION

Events, according to the type of theory defended here and the type of theory that has been defended by Kim, are one-time things; they do not recur. The two theories, therefore, are inconsistent with the Humean theory of causation, according to which the causal relation is a matter of the *constant conjunction* of events: "One event causes another provided that whenever the first occurs, the second also occurs."

An adequate view of causation requires us to view it *nomologically,* by reference to laws of nature.[9] Thus, we have taken "It is a law of nature that   " as one of our undefined philosophical locutions. The concept is analogous to that expressed by "It is a law of logic that   ."

If it is a law of logic that if A then B, then conceivably a rational being could know a priori, just by reflection, that it must be the case that if A occurs, then B occurs. But laws of nature can be ascertained only as a result of empirical investigation and not a priori.

Making use of our undefined concept of a law of nature, we shall introduce the concept of a *sufficient causal condition.*

We have, then, a number of tasks. One is to define the appropriate sense of sufficient causal condition. Another is to define *partial cause.* In the course of doing so, we will encounter a number of difficult philosophical questions.

Following is our definition of the concept of a sufficient causal condition:

> D14   S is a sufficient causal condition of E =Df
> S is a set of events that is such that it is
> causally but not logically necessary that E
> occurs either when all the members of S
> occur or later

We speak of events *occurring* rather than *existing,* for this is the more natural way to speak. But according to our theory of events, there are no events that do not occur.

Consider the example of a fire that occurs while a bird happens to be singing. The singing of the bird, we assume, plays no role in the causation of the fire. It is essential, therefore, that our explication does not inadvertently assign a causal role to the singing.[10]

How can we ensure that the singing of the bird is not one of the members of a sufficient causal condition of the fire? Our definition of sufficient causal condition allows for superfluous members – members that cannot be said in any sense to contribute causally to the effect. This fact suggests the possibility of singling out a *minimal* sufficient causal condition having no superfluous members.

We want a definition of minimal sufficient causal condition that will be such that, in its application to the example of the fire, it will not include the event that is the bird singing. We propose, then, the following:

> D15   S is a minimal sufficient causal condition
> of E =Df (1) S is a sufficient causal condi-
> tion of E; and (2) no subset of S is a suffi-
> cient causal condition of E

This definition rules out the possibility that one of the members of S is the following event:

(W): The bird being such that it is singing; and if it is singing, then the fire occurs.

81

The event W logically implies the singing of the bird.

Thus, because S is a minimal sufficient causal condition of the fire, S cannot have W as a member. For if S did have W as a member, S would not be a sufficient causal condition of the fire. Now we can define a *partial cause:*

> D16   C is a partial cause of E =Df C is a member
> of a minimal sufficient causal condition
> of E

Those events that *contribute causally* to the occurrence of an event E are partial causes of E, sets of partial causes of E, and sufficient causal conditions of E.

Any discussion of the nature of causation should be adequate to the possibility that some events have no sufficient causal conditions. For no one knows whether every event has a sufficient causal condition.

Let us say that an event having a sufficient causal condition is an event that is causally *determined* and that an event that has no sufficient causal condition is an event that is causally *undetermined.* May an event that is causally undetermined have *partial causes?* I shall now describe the conditions under which an undetermined event would have partial causes.

Suppose that your moving toward the right is undetermined. If your moving in some direction or other *is* determined, then whatever contributes causally to the latter determined event also contributes causally to the former undetermined event. How, then, is it possible to contribute causally to an undetermined event?

We first give definitions for (proper) parthood of events. Our definitions conform to D8 and D9.

> D17   The content of event E is part of the con-
> tent of event H =Df The content of H im-
> plies the content of E; and the content of
> E does not imply the content of H

D18   Event E is part of event H =Df Either (1)
the substrate of event E is a proper part of
the substrate of event H; or (2) the content
of event E is part of the content of event H

We may now say that whatever contributes causally to any
event contributes causally to any part of that event. If your
moving in some direction or other is determined and if your
moving toward the right is undetermined, then whatever contributes causally to the former determined event also contributes causally to the latter undetermined event.

What we say is not restricted to human actions. It may be
that the fire of our earlier example was determined to begin
within 30 minutes after the reappearance of the sun but not
within 15 minutes after its reappearance. If the fire does begin
15 minutes after the reappearance of the sun, then whatever
contributed causally to the former determined event contributed causally to the latter undetermined event.

Hence, no difficulties are involved in saying that undetermined events may have partial causes.

We turn, finally, to a slightly different question. Some events
are "overdetermined." They have more contributing causes
than they need. Does this fact constitute a difficulty for our
analysis of causation? A single example will suffice.

Two marksmen shoot at the victim; they are each successful,
and the two shots do their work at precisely the same time.
Given the one shot, the other shot was not needed to bring
about the effect. Both shots, therefore, would not be part of a
minimal sufficient causal condition, yet each contributed.
Should we, therefore, revise the definition of a minimal sufficient causal condition?

We do not need to revise the definition. It is a mistake to
assume that if there is a minimal causal condition for a certain
effect, then there is only *one* minimal causal condition for that
effect. In the case of the two shots, there are two minimal
causal conditions – one that includes one of the shots and a

second that includes the other. Hence, we may say that each shot contributed to the effect.

The fact that some events are overdetermined, then, does not require us to revise our analysis of causation.

11

SPATIAL ENTITIES AND MATERIAL SUBSTANCE

INTRODUCTION

We turn now to those contingent things that are not states. All such entities, according to the theory of categories that is being developed here, are individual things. We may define the concept of a *material* substance by reference to the concept of a *spatial* substance. We shall define the concept of a spatial substance by reference to *boundaries*. And we shall conclude that familiar physical things *are* material substances in the sense to be thus singled out.

SPATIAL COINCIDENCE

If there are scattered spatial things, then there are unscattered continuous material things. How could there be any scattered things if there were no unscattered things? For simplicity of exposition, we pretend that an ordinary block of wood is a continuous spatial object. The fact that, despite appearances, the block of wood is scattered, rather than continuous, is not relevant to the point of the example. It may be that the non-scattered constituents of material things do not include any of those constituents that are familiar to us. Which material things, then, are unscattered? We shall return to this question later when we consider the question: Which things are spatial substances?

If the block is a continuous spatial object, then every (proper) part of the block is in contact with another part of the block. And if the block has constituents that are not three-dimensional, then between any two such constituents there are still others. If, say, the block contains two-dimensional slices, then between any two such slices there are other slices. The series of slices within such a continuous object is *dense*, just as the series of fractions is dense. Between any two, no matter how close they may be, there are still others.

The top half of the block has, among its parts, a left half and a right half; it also has a top half and a bottom half. And it has, as parts, the *parts* of those parts – the halves of those halves. (I note once again that *part* is here taken to mean the same as what is usually intended by *proper part*.) If a thing is a continuous spatial object, then it is logically possible to divide the thing into halves, then to divide each half into further halves, and so on, ad indefinitum.

We thus encounter the ancient philosophical question: Is it logically possible to divide *every* part of the block? What would the result be? What would be left? Aristotle puts the problem this way:

> To suppose that a body (i.e., a magnitude) is divisible through and through, and that this division is possible, involves a difficulty. . . . If it is divisible through and through, and if this division is possible, then it might *be*, at one and the same moment, *divided* through and through. . . . What will then remain? A magnitude? No; that is impossible, since there will be something not divided. . . . The [former] constituents of the body will *either* be points (i.e., without magnitude) *or* absolutely nothing. If its [former] constituents are nothings, then it might both come-to-be out of nothing or exist as a composite of nothings. . . . But if it consists of points a similar absurdity will result. . . . Even if all the points are put together, they will not make any magnitude.[1]

St. Thomas Aquinas, in commenting on Aristotle's discussion, observes that "a thing is generated out of that into which it is resolved."[2] His point is that if a thing can be decomposed in such a way that no former parts of the thing remain in existence, then the thing can be *constructed out of* nothing. And this, St. Thomas says, is absurd. Surely he is right. Each part of a spatial object is divisible into smaller parts, and no matter how long we continue to divide, we will be left with parts that can be divided once again.

But from the fact that each part of a three-dimensional spatial object has still other parts, we should not infer, as we may be tempted to do, that every constituent of that object is itself a three-dimensional spatial object. Any adequate account of the matter would require us to say that spatial objects have points, lines, and surfaces as constituents. And points, lines, and surfaces are not three-dimensional physical bodies.

THE PROBLEM OF INNER SPATIAL CONTACT

To describe spatial contact, we should consider the nature of *inner* spatial contact – the contact that relates the inner parts and other constituents of a spatial body. The constituents that exist within a continuous body are such that each is in *indirect* contact with *all* of the others and each is in *direct* contact with *some* of the others.

Suppose that the piece of wood we have been considering is an ordinary ruler. What is involved in saying that the first half of the ruler is in contact with the second? Our first thought may be that the far end of the first half *touches* the near end of the second. But this will not do. Since the first half has a far end and the second half has a near end, then there are *two* inner surfaces, the one being an inner surface of the first half and the other being an inner surface of the second half. From the fact that the first half is in contact with the second, we may draw the following conclusions: Either (1) the first of the two surfaces is exactly where the second is or (2) there are indefinitely many other surfaces *between* the first and the second. In the first case, two entirely different things would be in exactly the same place. And in the second case, we cannot say that the one is the far end of the first half and the other is the near end of the second half.

We now attempt to develop the present approach more exactly and systematically.

Basic mereological concepts and axioms

We begin by locating the relevant concepts within the general theory of categories that has been set forth.

D1   x is a *contingent individual* =Df (1) x is a contingent thing; and (2) x is not a state of anything

D2   x is a *boundary* of, or in, y =Df x is necessarily such that it is a constituent of y

If a thing x is a *constituent* of a thing y, then x is also a (*proper*) *constituent of a constituent* of y.[3] It is essential that the definiens not be read as "a constituent of y is necessarily such that x is a constituent of *it*."

D3   x is a *contingent substance* =Df (1) x is a contingent individual; and (2) x is not a boundary

We may now characterize *parts* as being a subcategory of *constituents*.

D4   x is *part* of y =Df (1) x is a constituent of y; and (2) x is not a boundary

Turning to the undefined concept expressed by "x is a constituent of y," we formulate three axioms that are typical of *mereology*, the theory of part and whole.[4]

A1   For every x, y, and z, if x is a constituent of y and if y is a constituent of z, then x is a constituent of z

A2   For every x and y, if x is a constituent of
       y, then y is not a constituent of x

We are thus using *constituent* in the sense of *proper constituent.*
In this sense, we cannot say of anything that it is a constituent
of itself.

Next, we formulate what seems to me to be the clearest version of the *infinite divisibility* principle:

A3   For every x and y, if x is a constituent of
       y, then y has a constituent that has no
       constituents in common with x

From this principle, it follows that there can be no smallest
spatial continuum. Every spatial continuum, no matter how
small it may be, has constituents that are even smaller.

Spatial dimensions

Aristotle said that one thing is in spatial *contact* with another
thing provided that an extremity of the one is in the same
place as an extremity of the other. He said further that one
thing is spatially *continuous* with another thing provided that
an extremity of the one thing is "one with" an extremity of
the other. This view might tempt some to infer, incorrectly,
that an extremity of the one *becomes identical to* an extremity of
the other.[5] Suppose that A is not now identical to B and that
B will endure for the remainder of the year. If A is not now
identical to B, it is now such that it will not share B's history
after tomorrow; but if A becomes identical to B tomorrow,
then A will be such that it does share B's history for the rest of
the year, which is absurd. But all the distinctions to which we
appeal here were well known to Aristotle. One should, therefore, look for some other interpretation of the expression "to
become one with." These historical questions, however, are
not our present concern.

   I suggest the following explication of spatial dimensions,

which is in the spirit of the views we have just referred to. (We say something is a boundary if and only if it is a boundary of something.)

> D5   x is a *surface* =Df (1) x is a boundary; and
> (2) x is possibly such that it is not a con-
> stituent of a boundary

The total outer surface of a continuous body is not a constituent of anything.

> D6   x is a spatial *point* =Df (1) x is a boundary;
> and (2) x is not possibly such that it has
> a constituent

> D7   x is a *line* =Df (1) x is a boundary; (2) x
> has constituents; and (3) x is not a surface

Nothing that is a surface is a line, and nothing that is a line is a point. Thus, the classes of surfaces, lines, and points are mutually exclusive.

THE COINCIDENCE OF SPATIAL BOUNDARIES

We turn now to the coincidence of spatial boundaries. Here we make use of our spatial primitive: "x spatially overlaps with y."

> D8   x is a *spatial object* =Df x spatially overlaps
> with something other than itself

> A4   For every x, if x is a spatial object, then
> either (1) x has a surface or (2) x is a sur-
> face, line, or point

> D9   x stands in the relationship of *total coinci-
> dence* to y =Df Every constituent of x over-
> laps spatially with a constituent of y

> A5   For every x, x is possibly such that it
> stands in the relation of total coincidence
> to something other than itself if and only
> if x is a surface, line, or point

Our assumptions imply that there *are* things that stand in the relation of total coincidence.

If two different boundaries can exist in exactly the same place, then it is very difficult to avoid the conclusion that still other boundaries may also exist where they are. Brentano tells us that Galileo had seen this fact:

> Galileo . . . drew attention to the fact that the mid-point of a circle allows the distinction of just as many parts as there are points on the circumference, since it differs in a certain sense as starting-point of the different individual radii. If a red and [a] blue surface are in contact with each other, then a red and a blue line coincide. . . . And if a circular area is made of three sectors, a red, a blue and a yellow, then the mid-point is a whole which consists to an equal extent of a red, a blue and a yellow part.[6]

Hence we do not say that *whatever is colored is extended.* Suppose that everything colored were extended. Then a red surface would be such that not one of its constituent points is red. How could that be if the entire surface is red? What we should say is not that whatever is colored is extended, but rather that *whatever is colored is either extended or a constituent of something that is extended.*

CONTACT BETWEEN SPATIAL OBJECTS

We considered a ruler, so viewed that the first inch is the nearest inch. The farthest boundary of the first inch spatially coincides with the nearest boundary of the second inch. Therefore, the first inch is in *direct contact* with the second; the first inch is also in direct contact with the remainder of the ruler; it is in contact, but not in direct contact, with the third inch and with every spatial constituent beyond the third inch. Although the first inch is not itself in direct contact with the third, it is in direct contact with something that *is* in direct contact with the third.

Direct spatial contact may be explicated in the following way by reference to total spatial coincidence:

> D10   x is in *direct spatial contact* with y =Df A constituent of x coincides spatially with a constituent of y

Our terminology allows us to say that all spatial individuals coincide spatially with themselves.

We have said that all of the constituents of our ruler are in spatial contact with each other, even though not all are in direct spatial contact with each other. We may explicate the general concept of spatial contact in terms of direct spatial contact. To do this, we use the method Frege used to define the mathematical concept of successor in terms of the concept of direct spatial successor.[7]

> D11   x is in *spatial contact* with y =Df x is contained in every class C that contains y and anything that is in direct spatial contact with any member of C

A thing that turns back on itself (e.g., a tire, a hoop, or a doughnut) is in contact with itself. Lines and surfaces can turn back on themselves.

SPATIAL CONTINUITY

To explain what we here understand by *spatial continuity,* we use the concept of a spatial object introduced in definition D8.

> x is a *spatial object* =Df x is spatially continuous with something other than itself

Some spatial objects are scattered objects and others are unscattered objects. An unscattered spatial object is a continuous spatial object.

> D12   x is a *continuous spatial object* =Df (1) x is a spatial object; (2) x has constituents; and

(3) every constituent of x is in spatial contact with another constituent of x

A continuous spatial individual is an object that is not scattered. But it is consistent with our definition to say that a continuous spatial individual has *holes* in it, just as a piece of Swiss
cheese has holes.

A6   For every x, if x is a continuous spatial individual, then every constituent of x is either a spatial boundary or a continuous
spatial individual

A spatial point is not a continuous individual.

Our principle implies that the *temporal parts* of the *history* of
an individual are not parts of the substance itself. For the parts
of the history of an individual are parts of a *state*, not parts of
an individual. (This conclusion has been denied, at least im-
plicitly, by a number of contemporary philosophers.) But those
individual things that are *entia successiva* (things having parts at
one time that they lack at other times) may have individual
things as temporal parts.[8]

SPATIAL SUBSTANCES

D13   x is a *spatial substance* =Df x is a spatial object that is not a boundary

Our scheme should have a place for nonspatial substances:

D14   x is a *nonspatial substance* =Df x is a substance that is not a spatial substance

What would be an example of a nonspatial substance? If
there are thinking substances that are *monads*, such entities
would be nonspatial substances. We should resist the tempta-
tion to call these entities *mental substances*, for "mental" might

93

here suggest *mental stuff*. But one might call them *non-material substances*.

To ask "What is the 'nature' of that physical thing?" is to ask *what type of stuff* it has. It is for the natural sciences – physics, chemistry, and biology – to tell us about the nature of the various types of stuff and to explain the results of combining things of different stuffs.[9] The physical nature of a material thing depends on the nature of the parts that that thing is composed of and on the relations among those parts.[10]

We have not yet encountered any reason for thinking that there is a "mind stuff" that is both nonmaterial and nonspatial. It would seem, then, that all and only spatial substances are material substances.

WHICH THINGS ARE SPATIAL SUBSTANCES?

Physics tells us that the familiar material things we know, such "macroscopic objects" as sticks, stones, trees, and houses, are spatially scattered objects. It also tells us that atoms, once thought to be the smallest parts of matter, are scattered objects composed of such things as protons and neutrons. But it would be a mistake to suppose that physics tells us that *all* material things are scattered objects.

The investigations of physics presuppose that matter has *mass*. The general point may be put, somewhat loosely, by saying that all material things are made up of things that have mass.

We have asked: "Which material things are spatial substances?" The answer is: "Those material things that have mass." And *which* material things have mass? This is a question of physics, not of philosophy. Some physicists describe the ultimate constituents of matter as consisting of "strings" or "superstrings." These entities would have the spatial continuity that we have tried to describe.[11]

CONFIRMING THE PRESENT APPROACH: ANOTHER PUZZLE

Recent investigations involving the problem of contact seem to have left the general situation unchanged. This is confirmed by a recent study on the problem of collision by David Kline and Carl A. Matheson.[12] Their primary concern is with the possibility of collision, but since collision implies contact, they also discuss the problem of contact. And what they say is relevant to what we have said about spatial boundaries.

They argue as follows:

(1) If two bodies are touching, then they either occupy adjacent points in space or they overlap spatially.
(2) Space is continuous.
(3) No two bodies can ever occupy adjacent points in space. (Since space is continuous, no spatial point is ever adjacent to another spatial point.)
(4) It is impossible for two material bodies to overlap spatially.
(5) Therefore, no two bodies ever touch.[13]

The authors say that the concept of spatial contact involves the following difficulty: Although no two physical objects can share a region of *nonzero* spatial volume, boundaries of two physical objects can share a region of *zero* physical volume. This is "utterly mysterious."

If we could show that boundaries are not physical objects, then, of course, we would have a reply to the objection. For we could say that although no two physical objects can share a region of zero physical volume, two boundaries *can* share such a region. Hence we need to offer a reason for asserting that spatial boundaries of physical objects are not themselves physical objects.

Is there a property that is such that we would all agree (1) that no physical object has that property and (2) that every boundary has that property? We have been discussing such a property.

Consider this fact: No physical object is necessarily such that it is a proper part of a larger physical object. So far as the principles of logic and mereology are concerned, any physical object could have been "the only physical object there is." More exactly, any physical object x is possibly such that every physical object is identical either to x or to a constituent of x.

We have, then, the following argument:

(1) No physical object x is necessarily such that it is a constituent of another physical object.

The second premise tells us, in effect, that spatial boundaries have a property that is contrary to the property just attributed to physical objects; boundaries must be constituents of physical objects.

(2) Every spatial boundary is necessarily such that there is some physical object that contains it as a constituent.

Therefore:

(3) No spatial boundary is a physical object.

If we wish to defend the possibility of spatial contact, then, we do not need to deny any generally accepted thesis of physics. We need only show that boundaries are ontologically dependent in the sense that we have discussed. And isn't it more plausible to assume that boundaries *are* thus dependent than to assume that the possibility of physical contact is doubtful?[14]

THE PLACE OF SUBSTANCES

Does the existence of spatial substances presuppose a *space* in which such substances exist? And is this space still another entity to be added to our list of categories?

We identify *places* by reference to the *individuals* that are said to occupy those places. We also identify some places by reference to still other places. But every place that we thus identify

is, in the final analysis, identified by reference to the individuals that are said to be located *in* that place. Cities and their
suburbs are instances of what we commonly call places. We
may identify a suburb by reference to the city of which it is a
part. And as for identifying a city, we may do so by reference
to the hills, mountains, or rivers that are, even if only for a
relatively short time, to be found there. In such cases, we
would then proceed in the wrong direction if we sought to
identify the hills, mountains, or rivers by reference to their
places.[15]

"But whenever we find ourselves identifying an *individual
thing*, we can always go on and identify that thing by reference
to its place *in space*" (emphasis added). As Leibniz pointed out,
the entities that are available to us, so far as *places in space* are
concerned, are *the spatial relations* that obtain between spatial
bodies (emphasis added). He wrote:

> I hold *space* to be something *merely relative*, as *time* is; . . . I hold
> it to be an *order of coexistences*, as *time* is an *order of successions*. For
> *space* denotes, in terms of possibility, *an order* of things which
> exist at the same time, considered as existing *together*, without
> inquiring into their particular manner of existing. And when
> many things are seen *together*, one perceives *that order of things*
> among "*themselves*."[16]

Leibniz also observed: "I don't say that matter and space are
the same thing. I only say, where there is no space there is
no matter."[17]

From the point of view of the present theory of categories,
however, it is better to say that there is space only if there are
spatial objects – just as we have said that there is no temporal
duration unless there are events.

12

PERSONS AND THEIR BODIES: SOME UNANSWERED QUESTIONS

Having considered the nature of material bodies, we are naturally led to consider the ancient questions concerning the relations between *persons* and their bodies. The theory of categories does not, as such, provide answers to these questions, but it does provide an instructive perspective from which to consider them. I now consider these questions from that perspective.

I recall some of the considerations that have led philosophers to conclude that persons are simple substances.

THREE POSSIBLE VIEWS

Using the first person, I will begin with the question "What is the relation between me and my body?" Among the various possible views, there are three to be considered seriously: (1) that I am identical to my body; (2) that I am a simple substance without bodily parts; and (3) that I am a proper part of this body. (There would seem to be no good reason for thinking that I might be identical to a bodily aggregate having proper parts that are *not* now parts of my present body.)

(1) First, there is the view that I am identical to my body. One may argue that since many of these bodily parts are such that I could readily dispense with them, I could hardly be identical to the total set of such parts. More important, however, is the fact that throughout my life, my body is in flux in a way

in which I myself cannot be said to be in flux. This fact has suggested to many that whereas one's body persists through time in only a loose and popular sense, the person persists in a strict and philosophical sense. If this reasoning is sound, then the person is not to be identified with his or her body.

(2) There is the view that I am a substance that is *not a bodily substance* – in which case, I am a *simple substance*, or *monad*.

(3) Finally, there is the view that I am identical to a proper part of my body. We will call the acceptance of this possibility the *bodily part view*. This view enables us to make the following distinction: One could hold that although the gross body persists only in a loose and popular sense, that proper part that is oneself exists in a strict and philosophical sense. In such a case, the fate of the smaller part may be independent of that of the larger body.

Considerations that tend to favor the simple substance view may readily be adapted to the bodily part view. In some cases, the attempted proofs of simplicity may seem to gain plausibility when so adapted. The view that persons are simple substances, or monads, has been defended by some of the great figures in the history of Western philosophy. (But, it should be added, there do not seem to be many authorities who recommend the bodily part view.)

How would one defend the view according to which each person is a simple substance? We now consider two arguments that have been or can be used to support such a conclusion. One of the arguments is from Kant; the other is from Maimonides.

An argument adapted from Kant

Kant presents this argument in the second of his supposed "paralogisms of transcendental psychology." He formulates the argument this way:

That, the action of which can never be regarded as the concurrence of several things, is *simple*.
  Now the soul, or the thinking "I," is such a thing.
  Therefore, etc.[1]

Kant insists that the argument "is no mere sophistical play . . . but an inference that appears to withstand even the closest scrutiny" (A351). Then he goes on to say:

> Suppose a compound thing were to think. Then every part of that compound would have a part of that thought. The thought that the compound would then have would be composed of the thoughts of the parts of that compound. But this would be contradictory. For thoughts that are distributed among different thinkers can never constitute a single thought. From the fact that the different words of a piece of poetry are thought of by different thinkers it does not follow that the aggregate of those thinkers has thought of the piece of poetry. It is, therefore, impossible for an aggregate to think. (A352)

Given this reasoning, it would be a simple matter to complete the argument:

  I think; therefore, I am not a compound.

Whatever Kant himself may have intended, his reasoning has some plausibility if it is spelled out in the following way: We consider a compound substance and a compound thought. The compound substance has three parts: A, B, and C. And the compound thought has three parts: (p) that Dion is walking, (q) that wheat is being sold on the market, and (r) that Dion needs to buy some wheat. We suppose that there is a unique connection between A and p: A is that part of the thinking subject that thinks p. And analogously for the other two cases: B is that part of the thinking subject that thinks q, and C is that part of the thinking subject that thinks r. In such a case, the compound subject could be said to be the subject of a compound thought.
  But if this is the way compounds may be said to think, then

let us now abstract from those of one's bodily parts, whatever they may be, that do *not* thus contribute to one's thinking. We then consider just the parts that remain. Returning to our example, consider part A, which serves as the subject of the thought (p) that Dion is walking. *It* has no parts that constitute the subject of *that* thought. For that thought is not compound. Does this present us with a good reason to say that A is a simple substance? Or can it be used equally well to support the bodily part view?

An argument adapted from Maimonides

The second argument is suggested in the *Guide to the Perplexed* by Moses Maimonides. In discussing the incorporeality of God, Maimonides formulates – and rejects – an argument that could readily be restated as an argument for the simplicity of the soul. It is this:

> If God were corporeal, His true essence would necessarily either exist entirely in every part of the body, that is to say, in each of its atoms, or would be confined to one of the atoms. In the latter alternative the other atoms would be superfluous, and the existence of the corporeal being [with the exception of the one atom] would be of no purpose. If, on the other hand, each atom fully represented the Divine Being, the whole body would not be *one* deity, but a complex of deities, and this would be contrary to the doctrine adopted by the *kalâm* that God is one.[2]

Maimonides rejects this argument on the ground that it has a false presupposition – namely, that God is composed of atoms. But in application to persons other than the deity, it has at least the following plausibility:

Consider the hypothesis according to which the person is identical to some extended proper part P of his or her body. However small P may be, there is no sufficient reason for supposing that P itself, rather than some proper part of P, is identical to that person. And so, to the question "How small could I be?", the answer would seem to be "Smaller than any dimension that one can specify."

Maimonides's argument, so interpreted, is thus very similar to the argument we have attributed to Kant.

We are left, then, with a difficult choice – that between saying (1) that we are very small physical substances and saying (2) that we are substances that are so small that we have no parts at all. Is a simple substance *too* small? How does it differ from nothing at all?

One would like to find a way out.

The bundle theory of the self

Consider the following philosophical maxim: "The statement of a philosophical theory should await the completion of any philosophical program that might show the theory to be inadequate." If we were to follow that maxim, there would be no progress in philosophy. But if the philosophical program is, prima facie, more plausible than the theory, then the commonsense approach would be to consider the proposal before trying to develop the theory. Or if we wish to persuade others, we may be interested in showing *them* the difficulties that the program involves.

"After all," the bundle theorist may say, "what we say implies only that there are classes or sets and that there are attributes. And classes or sets are reducible to attributes. Hence, we can reject *substantialism,* and therefore we do not need to assume that there *is* such a thing as the self or subject."

The situation, however, is not so simple. Brentano remarked, in his lectures on descriptive psychology, that the concept of a *bundle,* if it is to serve its purpose, requires not only the concepts of the items that are bundled, but also the concept of "a cord or wire, or the like, that ties things together."[3] What he had in mind may be suggested by the following.

Consider the bundles of attributes that are those of two different selves, T and C. The two bundles will comprise such attributes as the following:

T	C
being joyful	being sad
hoping for rain	hoping for no rain
having a red sensation	having a blue sensation
thinking of walking	thinking of eating

The bundle theorist would like to say: "Here we have just two sets of attributes, T and C. We don't need to appeal to any entities other than to *attributes* and to *sets* of attributes."

But there are *more* than two sets of attributes here; indeed, there are many more. Thus, there are also these sets of attributes:

D	E
being joyful	being sad
having a blue sensation	having a red sensation
thinking of eating	thinking of walking

Sets T and C could be said to be *genuine* bundles and sets D and E *defective* bundles. And so, we may point out to the bundle theorist: "Not every bundle of attributes constitutes a self. For clearly, defective bundles such as D and C do not constitute selves. What, then, is the distinction between the genuine bundles and the defective ones?"

We may say: "What makes T and C genuine bundles is the fact that each is a set of attributes all belonging to the *same self.*" But this answer is not available to the bundle theorist.

Could he or she say that a genuine bundle is a set of attributes all occupying one *place?* Then the bundle theorist would have given up the simple ontology with which he or she had hoped to begin. We would be saying that, in addition to attributes, there are *places,* and that attributes may be located in these places.

An ontology that assigned attributes to places in absolute space would be very different from the theory of categories that has been developed here.

PART THREE

Homeless Objects

. .

13

APPEARANCES

Merely by varying the conditions under which a physical thing is perceived, one may vary the appearances that that thing will present. I say that one may do this merely by varying the conditions under which the thing is perceived. One does not need to introduce any changes in the thing itself. The time-honored – or notorious – examples of the epistemologist are designed to bear this out. These include the stick that is made to look bent merely by immersing it in water and the white cloth that is made to appear pink merely by looking at it through rose-colored glasses.

Are *appearances* included among the individual things that have been provided for in our scheme of categories? Or are they another type of thing? We here defend the view that appearances are individual things.[1] They are sensed by the subject of experience. There are only two other possibilities. One is that appearances are *states;* the other is that they are *attributes.*

Normally, philosophers are concerned with the *qualitative* nature of appearances – with colors, sounds, tastes, smells, feels, hence the use of terms such as *sense qualities* and *qualia.* Our concern is with ontology and with the fact that, of all the possible hypotheses about the nature of appearances, the most plausible is the hypothesis that appearances are *individual things* of a *spatial* nature.

THE SPATIAL PROPERTIES OF APPEARANCES

One of the pre-analytic data of our problem is the fact that there are truths of the following sort:

> I sense an appearance that consists of a triangular red thing being to the left of a circular blue thing.

It is easy to imagine a situation in which one would sense such a spatial appearance.

Consider the hypothesis that the objects of visual sensing are *surfaces* within *the subject's own body*. This hypothesis does not require us to say that the subject is identical to his or her body. Nor does it require us to say that the subject is *not* identical with his or her body. But the hypothesis implies that the subject needs a body in order to sense.

The hypothesis enables us to deal easily with the example of the spatial nature of sensing. We may say that what the subject is sensing contains a red triangle being to the left of a blue circle. What is being sensed is a constituent of one of the body's surfaces.[2]

The objects of visual sensing are certainly spatial. Either (1) *all* objects of sensing are individual things or (2) *some* objects of sensing are individual things and *others* are of a quite different sort (e.g., attributes or states). The first hypothesis is simpler and is consistent with everything we know. We defend the view that the objects of *sensing* are surfaces, whereas the objects of *perception* are substances.

In the nineteenth century, Thomas Case defended a theory according to which the object of supposed external perception is always part of one's own nervous system.[3] The view was easily ridiculed: "You are telling us that whenever we sense an appearance, we are appeared to by our own brains. So what we perceive is always our own insides!" But, as we shall see, the present hypothesis, which distinguishes carefully sensing and perceiving, does not have this consequence.

THE ROLE OF APPEARANCES IN EXTERNAL AND
INTERNAL PERCEPTION

We begin with a notational abbreviation.

> D1   S's sensing of an appearance A is condi-
> tioned by O =Df (1) S senses an appear-
> ance A; and (2) the internal properties of
> A are causally conditioned by those of O

Following our definition D5 of Chapter 10, we say that being-
F is an *internal property* of a thing x, provided only that x is F
and has every property that being-F implies. If one property is
thus causally dependent on another, then variations in the first
property are causally dependent on variations in the second.

> D2   S perceives an external substance O =Df
> (1) S's sensing of an appearance A is con-
> ditioned by O; (2) O is a substance that is
> external to S's body; and (3) there is no M
> such that (a) M is external to S's body, (b)
> M is entirely discrete from O, (c) S's sens-
> ing of A is conditioned by M, and (d) S's
> sensing of O is conditioned by M

Two individual things are *entirely discrete* from each other if
they have no constituents in common.

Our definition has the consequence that if you see a person's
reflection in a mirror or hear the person's voice on the tele-
phone, you do not thereby *perceive* the person. But this consequence is innocuous.

There is a *propositional* sense of *perceive,* as in "S perceives
that there is a tree." And there is a *nonpropositional sense,* as
in "S perceives a tree." Definition D2 is concerned with the
nonpropositional sense of *perception.* And it is presupposed by the
propositional sense of perception ("S *perceives that* x is F").

The propositional sense of *perceives* has two features that are
not shared by the nonpropositional sense ("S perceives x"): (1)

It is *doxastic* in that it implies a belief about the appearance and the perceived object. (2) It is *epistemic* in that it implies that the belief about the appearance and the object is one that is *epistemically justified* for the perceiver.[4]

The nonpropositional sense of *internal* bodily perception is completely analogous to that of external perception. We may define it as follows:

> D3 S perceives a substance O within S's body =Df (1) S's sensing of an appearance A is conditioned by O; (2) O is a substance that is internal to S's body; and (3) there is no M such that (a) M is internal to S's body, (b) M is entirely discrete from O, (c) S's sensing of A is conditioned by M, and (d) S's sensing of O is conditioned by M

In this way, we describe the role of appearances in perception. What we have said provides for the possibility of both external and internal perception. And it does not require us to add to our list of categories.

THE EXISTENCE OF QUALITIES

In our concern to do justice to the spatial nature of sensing, we must not lose sight of the fact that sensing is preeminently qualitative.

I do not hesitate to say that the qualitative nature of sensing is of cosmological significance. One could use Gustav Fechner's metaphor and say that the facts in question provide us with a "daylight view" of the world. The suggestion may be particularly tempting in connection with those acts that are qualitatively rich and pleasing. But other acts of sensing could be said, with equal justification, to provide us with a "dark and pain-ridden view of the world" – where the predicates "dark" and "pain-ridden" are taken in what we have called a positive and not merely a negative sense.[5]

13 Appearances

Our qualitative experience – the sensing of appearances – is subjective in being dependent for its existence on the existence of the sensing subject of experience. And perhaps it is well to add what should be obvious: The fact that there are sentient beings having such qualitative experiences *is* a fact – an objective fact – about the nature of this world.

14

INTENTIONALIA

Socrates: Does not he who thinks think some one thing?

Theaetetus: Certainly.

Soc: And does not he who thinks some one thing, think something which is?

Theaet: I agree.

Soc: Then he who thinks of that which is not thinks of nothing?

Theaet: Clearly.

Soc: And he who thinks of nothing does not think at all?

Theaet: Obviously.

–Plato[1]

INTRODUCTION

What we here call the problem of *intentionalia* has also been called the problem of *intentional inexistence* as well as the problem of *immanent objectivity*. It usually arises in connection with those thoughts that seem to take nonexistent individuals as their objects. One asks: "What is it to have a unicorn or a winged horse or a mermaid as the object of one's thought?"

115

EXAMPLES OF A PERSISTENT DOCTRINE

There is a clear statement of the doctrine of intentional inexistence in St. Augustine's treatise entitled "On the Soul and its Origin" (Book IV, Ch. 25). Augustine is concerned to refute the view according to which "where there are no bodies there is no assigning of names." He asks us to consider the objects we see in our dreams. Then he observes that "it is in fact mainly by these imaginary sights that the soul is proved to be incorporeal." He then concludes:

> Whoever takes these phantoms to be bodies is incredibly foolish; [they are not bodies], although they are certainly very like bodies. . . . Who can possibly trace out or describe the character or the material of which they consist? It is, beyond question, spiritual, not corporeal. If, therefore, the soul were a material body, it could not possibly contain so many things and such large forms of bodily substances in its scope of thought and in the spaces of its memory.[2]

In the seventeenth century, Descartes discusses essentially the same problem and adds very little to what Augustine had said about the ontological status of these nonbodily individuals. Descartes speaks of objects that exist "only in the mind" and says of them that they have a mode of being that is "truly much less perfect than that in which things exist outside the mind, but it is not on that account mere nothing."[3]

In the twentieth century, A. O. Lovejoy offers a version of Augustine's doctrine of intentional inexistence, saying that it is of fundamental importance to metaphysics. He uses it, just as Augustine had done, to defend an ontological dualism. "No man doubts," Lovejoy writes, "that when he brings to mind the look of a dog he owned when a boy, there is something of a canine sort" (something that is a dog?) "immediately present to and therefore compresent with his consciousness. And it is quite certainly not that dog in the flesh."[4] He goes on to say that the thing that is "of a canine sort" is not itself a physical object. It is an *individual thing*, presumably a dog, but only an *intentionally inexistent* individual thing.

THE MOVE FROM INTENTIONALIA TO INTENTIONS

There is certainly something strange about this type of onto-logical dualism. Brentano, who in the nineteenth century had reintroduced the concept of *intentional inexistence* into philoso-phy, came to see that the doctrine had consequences that are logically absurd. Suppose that one were to contemplate an im-possible individual – one that is both round and square. This supposition can hardly be taken to imply that there *is* some-thing, even a mentally dependent object, that is both round and square.[5]

Could it be, then, that the word *unicorn*, in such statements as "S is thinking about a unicorn," is not being used to desig-nate a unicorn at all? If we say this, then we should be able to give a positive account of the way in which the word *unicorn* *is* being used in such statements as "S is thinking about a unicorn."

Carnap had held briefly that it might be useful in philosophy to interpret the word *unicorn* in such psychological statements as designating the *word*. He suggested, more generally, that we might reformulate such statements as

Charles thinks (asserts, believes, wonders about) A

in the following way:

Charles thinks 'A.'[6]

The suggestion is not very plausible, however, as Carnap came to see. He was subsequently to view such statements as telling us not something about *words*, but something about the *attri-butes* that are *intended* by the relevant words in such state-ments. The view had also been suggested by Frege.[7] But just *what* does "S is thinking about a unicorn" tell us about the property or attribute of being a unicorn? Does the statement "S is thinking about a unicorn" really tell us that S is thinking about the property of being a unicorn?

Alonzo Church suggested that the sentence "Schliemann sought the site of Troy" tells us that a certain relation obtains between Schliemann and the *concept* of the site of Troy. The suggestion was that the act of *seeking* is a relation between a person and an *abstractum*. But what relation is asserted to obtain between Schliemann and the concept of the site of Troy? Schliemann was not seeking the concept, since it was necessary for him to have it in order to set out on his quest. Church says, negatively, that the relation that Schliemann bore to the concept of the site of Troy is "not quite like that of having sought," but he does not tell us more positively what it is.[8]

Before dealing positively with the ontological status of intentionalia, we consider briefly an influential alternative to the doctrine of intentional inexistence.

DEALING WITH INTENTIONALIA

Let us recall our intentional explication of the concept of an *attribute*. We had said this:

> D1 x has being-F as the intentional content
> of an act of believing =Df x believes that
> something is F

The key to the problem lies in the concept of the *content* of a thought; more accurately, it lies in the concept of an *act* of thinking. In discussing this concept, we have said that the content of an act of thinking is a property, or an attribute. The principal types of intentional act, as we have noted, may be suggested by these examples: believing or judging, that there is something that is F; trying or endeavoring to bring it about that something is F; desiring that there be something that is F; being favorably inclined toward there being something that is

F; being unfavorably inclined (or being disinclined) toward there being something that is F; and thinking about there being something that is F. All such acts may be said to be *directed* to an F. Trying, or endeavoring, is thus to be included among the psychological acts that have an intentional object.

Thus, we may add a further intentional explication:

> D2 x has being-F as the intentional content of
> an endeavor =Df x is endeavoring to bring
> it about that something is F

Schliemann, therefore, in seeking the site of Troy is endeavoring to bring it about that he, Schliemann, exemplifies the attribute of finding the site of Troy.

We may safely conclude, therefore, that facts about intentionally inexistent objects do not require the assumption that there is a special type of entity that exists only in the mind. There is nothing here that requires us to go beyond the present theory of categories.

15

FICTITIOUS OBJECTS

INTRODUCTION

We turn now to those things that are said to exist in the works of fiction. The problems are not quite the same as those involved in mentally inexistent objects. They are more simple in that if we formulate an adequate example, then the proper treatment of that one example will suffice in principle for any other example.[1] The following statement about Sherlock Holmes provides us with the example we need and will serve as a pre-analytic datum for our discussion.

> Sherlock Holmes is said to be (a) more famous than any actual detective, (b) smarter than Gulliver, (c) a fictional character, (d) Mary's favorite character, and (e) to have been created by Conan Doyle.[2]

What sort of entity does this statement describe?

STORIES AND THEIR CONTENTS

We deal with the problem by making use of the analyses of content, conceptual entailment, and assertion that we have already given. For present purposes, we will state the analyses this way:

D1   The property being-F is the *content* of one of x's thoughts =Df x thinks of there being something that is F

D2   The property being-F *conceptually entails* the property being-G =Df The property

being-F is necessarily such that whoever
has it as the content of a thought has the
property being-F as the content of a
thought

D3   x tells z a story that conceptually entails
that there is an F =Df x makes an utterance so that z will think of there being
something that is F

Still another formulation is: "x tells z a story that *purports to
attribute* the property of being F." We may say further: "If x has
a thought entailing that there is an F that has a certain name
N, then x thereby *interprets* N as the name of an F."

APPLICATION TO THE SHERLOCK HOLMES CASE

In what follows, we shall use "Holmes" as an abbreviation for
"Sherlock Holmes."

The application to the Sherlock Holmes case, as that case has
just been summarized, is fairly straightforward. The original
case could, of course, be described in more detail and with
finer nuances, and the application could then be revised accordingly.

We list, then, brief analyses of the more problematic types
of statement ostensibly describing fictitious objects. The analyses that appear earlier on the list are presupposed by those that
appear later.

A person S may be said to *tell a story* about a detective named
Holmes, provided that S makes an utterance in order to convey
the thought that there is a detective named Holmes. The kind
of thought conveyed in such cases is not belief but contempla-
tion or consideration.

To say that there is no detective who is as famous as Holmes
is to compare two numbers. (1) The first is the number of
people who interpret Holmes as the name of a detective; and
(2) the second is the number of people who interpret some

name other than Holmes as the name of a detective. The comparative statement tells us that the first number is larger than the second.

This account, it should be emphasized, does not require us to introduce a distinction between two types of detective – those that are actual and those that are fictitious.

To say, in the present context, that Holmes is Mary's favorite character is to say this: Of the two types of story, (1) those that are told in order to cause one to think of there being a detective named "Holmes" and (2) those that are told in order to cause one to think about something else instead, Mary prefers the former to the latter.

To say that the fictitious character named Holmes is *smarter than* the fictitious character named Gulliver is to say that the traits usually attributed to the character named Holmes are indicative of a higher degree of intelligence than the traits attributed to the character named Gulliver. Hence discussions about the psychological properties and complexes of fictitious characters *may* be as objective as discussions about those of nonfictitious characters.

Finally, saying that Conan Doyle "created" Holmes does not imply that Conan Doyle caused a fictitious entity to come into being. It tells us only that Conan Doyle was the first to tell a story implying that there is a detective named Holmes. (If it should turn out that someone else was the first to tell such a story, we would have to revise not the analysis that we have given, but the pre-analytic datum according to which Holmes was created by Conan Doyle.)

Statements ostensibly about fictitious objects, then, may be reduced to statements about those substances that are tellers of tales and about those substances who read or listen to those tales. Hence they do not raise a difficulty for the present theory of categories.

PART FOUR

Application to
Philosophical Theology

16

NECESSARY SUBSTANCE

What would a necessary substance be if there were such an entity? We want to answer the question within the scheme of concepts.

In discussing our undefined locution "x is necessarily such that it is F," we noted (1) that the schematic letter "F" may be replaced only by a predicate and (2) that "exists" is not a predicate. Hence, we cannot define a necessary substance as being "a substance that is necessarily such that it exists."

Consider once again the concepts of coming into being and passing away. In explicating these concepts, we said:

> D1   x is coming into being =Df x is such that there is nothing that it did exemplify

> D2   x is passing away =Df x is such that there is nothing that it will exemplify

We may now affirm the following:

> D3   x is a necessary substance =Df x is a substance that is not possibly such that it came into being or will pass away

A necessary substance, then, is an *eternal object*. In this respect, it is similar to attributes.

WOULD A NECESSARY BEING BE UNCHANGEABLE?

We have defended the thesis according to which everything is temporal. It follows from this thesis that even a necessary

127

substance is temporal and therefore subject to change. Consider Brentano's observation:

> If something changes, it follows that not all truths are eternal. God knows all truths and thus also those which are only today. These, however, he could not have known yesterday, since then it was not they, but certain others, which obtained. Thus he now knows for example that I am writing down these thoughts. Yesterday, however, he did not know this, but rather that I will write them down later. And similarly he will know tomorrow that I have written them down.[1]

But this view is difficult to reconcile with the thesis according to which temporal things are created by an unchangeable deity who "lives a motionless life [*totum simul*] where all is ever present." Boethius, from whom these words are quoted, makes the following suggestion:

> For the infinite notion of temporal things imitates the immediate present of His changeless life and, since it cannot reproduce or equal life, it sinks from immobility to motion and declines from the simplicity of the present into the infinite duration of future and past. And, since it cannot possess the whole fullness of its life at once, it seems to imitate to some extent that which it cannot completely express, and it does this by somehow never ceasing to be. It binds itself to a kind of present in this short and transitory period which, because it has a certain likeness to that abiding, unchanging present, gives everything it touches a semblance of existence. But, since this imitation cannot remain still, it hastens along the infinite road of time, and so it extends by movement the life whose completeness it could not achieve by standing still.[2]

The world of created things, Boethius here says, "*tries* to imitate the deity*"; it "*undertakes* an infinite journey through time." How are we to interpret these metaphorical statements? Can we interpret them in a way that does not personify the world of created things?

The only other possibility, it would seem, is to say that the intentions, ostensibly attributed to the created world, are to be attributed to God – to the unchangeable necessary substance that is said to have created those things. Such an answer would leave us with our philosophical problem – namely, that of explaining how the appearance of temporality can be attributed to the activity of an unchanging necessary substance.

THE ARGUMENT FROM DESIGN

The classic statement from design of the argument is the fifth of St. Thomas Aquinas's "five ways" of proving the existence of God.[3] He refers to it as the argument "from the governance of the world [*ex gubernatione rerum*]."

His formulation is this:

> The fifth way is taken from the governance of the world. We see that things, such as natural bodies, which lack intelligence act for an end, and this is evident from their acting always, or nearly always, in the same way, so as to obtain the best possible result [*aliquid est optimum*]. Hence it is plain that not fortuitously but designedly [*non a casu, sed ex intentione*], do they achieve their end. Now whatever lacks intelligence cannot move towards an end, unless it is directed by some being endowed with knowledge and intelligence [*nisi directa ab aliquo cognoscente et intelligente*], as the arrow is shot to its mark by the archer. Therefore some intelligent being [*aliquid intelligens*] exists by whom all natural things are directed to their end; and this being we call God.[4]

In appraising this argument, we should realize that Aquinas is concerned not merely with particular cases of ostensible purpose in nature, but also with *systems* or *chains* of such cases. He writes in the *Contra Gentes*:

> When diverse things are coordinated the scheme depends on their directed unification, as the order of battle of a whole army hangs on the plan of the commander-in-chief. The arrangement of diverse things cannot be dictated by their own private and divergent natures. . . . It follows that the order of many

among themselves is either a matter of chance or it must be resolved into one first planner who has a purpose in mind.[5]

Hence the expression "proof taken from the governance of the world."

IS THE HYPOTHESIS OF DESIGN
EPISTEMICALLY ACCEPTABLE?

Is the hypothesis of the divine governance of the world such that *not* accepting it is *not* more reasonable than accepting it? The question, which is epistemological, is best understood if we compare a parallel argument that *is* epistemically acceptable.

Alvin Plantinga set forth the following "tentative conclusion" at the end of his early work *God and Other Minds:* "if my belief in other minds is rational, so is my belief in God. But obviously the former is rational; so, therefore, is the latter."[6] Using the terminology that I have adopted in the present book and elsewhere, I would say that Plantinga was there arguing that the proposition that God exists is *not unreasonable;* and this, I think, we can certainly accept.

There is considerably more to be said.

BIOLOGICAL FUNCTION AND DESIGN

The kind of evidence to which St. Thomas Aquinas appeals, in his version of the argument from design, is recognized by most investigators of the relevant subject matter. But the ways of *describing* what the evidence is supposed to be evidence *for* differ significantly.

A prosaic example is less distracting than a more learned one. Let it be something like this:

> (D)   The liver of an organism secretes bile, with
>   the result that, under certain circum-

130

> stances, such and such a beneficial result
> occurs to that organism

(That the result in question itself seems designed to bring about a further result is not relevant to the present point.)

An investigator not concerned with theology or philosophy may not hesitate to formulate his conclusion this way:

(1) The *purpose* of the liver is to . . .

But we have put the conclusion this way:

(2) The liver is *designed* to . . .

The second formulation, unlike the first, may draw attention to the fact that if there is anything that can be said to serve a certain *purpose*, then there *is* something that – or who – *has* that purpose. The explicit reference to the designer may then be preserved, as it was by St. Thomas:

(3) There is an *intelligent being* who designed the liver to . . .

"And this being," St. Thomas goes on to say, "we call God."

Others will say, perhaps trying to proceed more cautiously:

(4) *Nature* designed the liver in such a way that it would . . .

"This is more cautious," they may explain, "because we all know that there *is* such an entity as nature."

Still others, more skeptical about the existence of a person who might be "Mother Nature," may prefer this:

(5) *Evolution* designed the liver in such a way that . . .

But here we have a category mistake par excellence. Evolution is a *process,* and processes are not the kinds of things that can be said to *think* or to *have plans and designs.* Substances, we have argued, are the only entities to which such activities may be attributed.

There seems to be only one remaining move. That is to reformulate the conclusion by removing the explicit reference to design and making use of the technical term *function*. One then says:

(6) The *function* of the liver is to . . .

But now the difficulty is that of distinguishing this final formula from the *data* (D), set forth above, that the formula is designed to explicate.[7]

The problem of finding a nonintentional interpretation of the biological term *function* is similar in all essential respects to that of finding a physicalistic explication of intentional concepts.

NOTES

Chapter 1

1. I have found J. L. Ackrill's account of Aristotle's theory especially helpful. I am referring in particular to the notes that he has provided for his edition of *Aristotle's Categories and De Interpretatione* (Oxford: Clarendon Press, 1963). Among useful discussions of such theories are Adolf Trendelenberg, *Geschichte der Kategorienlehre* (Berlin: Verlag von G. Bethge, 1846) and the article "Category" by Robert Adamson in the 11th edition of the *Encyclopaedia Britannica*, Vol. 5 (New York: Encyclopaedia Britannica Co., 1910), pp. 508–11.

2. Charles Sanders Peirce, *The Collected Papers of Charles Sanders Peirce* (Cambridge, Mass.: Harvard University Press, 1945), Vol. V, p. 100 (5.575). I have defended this general point of view in the third edition of *Theory of Knowledge* (Englewood Cliffs, N.J.: Prentice-Hall, 1989).

3. If we use the quantified modal logic developed by Ruth Barcan Marcus, then even though we may wish to affirm that "necessarily" implies "necessarily necessarily," we should take care not to use the "necessarily, for every x" of that system in such a way that the result implies "Necessarily, for every x, x is necessarily such that it is F," if the latter clause is taken in the way in which we are using it here. Compare R. C. Barcan, "A Functional Calculus of First Order Based on Strict Implication," *Journal of Symbolic Logic*, Vol. XI (1946), pp. 1–16. For a detailed account of the point that we have been discussing, see G. E. Hughes and M. J. Cresswell, *An Introduction to Modal Logic* (London: Methuen & Co., 1968), pp. 183–201. For a more general account of the philosophical significance of the relevant formal controversies, see Arthur Prior, *Formal Logic*, second edition (Oxford: Clarendon Press, 1962), pp. 185–229.

4. In saying at the outset that this book is not about *theories* of categories, I had in mind, in part, the difficulties that would be involved in doing justice within the scheme of the present book to such views as those of A. N. Whitehead. The most balanced account of Whitehead's views, so far as I know, is that of C. I. Lewis in "The Categories of Natural Knowledge," in J. D. Goheen and John L. Mothershead, eds., *Selected Papers of C. I. Lewis* (Stanford, Calif.: Stanford University Press, 1979), pp. 113–59. Lewis's paper first appeared in P. A. Schilpp, ed., *The Philosophy of Alfred North Whitehead*, Vol. III of the *Library of Living Philosophers* (La Salle, Ill.: Open Court Publishing Co.). This work was first published in 1941.

Chapter 2

1. W. V. Quine, *The Ways of Paradox and Other Essays* (New York: Random House, 1966), p. 15.
2. The example is from Jaegwon Kim. Kim has also called my attention to the possibility of strengthening the criterion of attribute identity. We could say that an attribute P and an attribute Q are identical just in case (a) they conceptually entail the same attributes and (b) they are conceptually entailed by the same attributes. But the weaker criterion is adequate for our purposes.
3. In this case, we should avoid using "is" to express the existential quantifier; we should say "There *exists* an x such that" and not "There *is* an x such that."
4. Compare Wittgenstein's observation: "It is easy to see that not all colour concepts are logically of the same sort, e.g., the difference between the concepts 'colour of gold' or 'colour of silver' and 'yellow' or 'grey.'" Ludwig Wittgenstein, *Remarks on Colour* (Berkeley: University of California Press, 1978), p. 9e.
5. They are discussed in more detail in my book *On Metaphysics* (Minnesota: University of Minnesota Press, 1989), chapter six.

Chapter 3

1. This type of criterion was first clearly formulated by W. V. Quine. See his essay "On What There Is," reprinted in his book *From a Logical Point of View* (New York: Harper & Row, 1961), pp. 1–19.

Chapter 4

1. I am indebted to Matt McGrath for suggesting a way to improve an earlier version of D1. The use of "being such that p" in this context was suggested to me by Ernest Sosa.
2. See his discussion of the ontological argument for the existence of God in the *Critique of Pure Reason*. See Norman Kemp Smith, ed., *Kant's Critique of Pure Reason* (London: Macmillan, 1933), pp. 599ff. Compare G. E. Moore's "Is Existence a Predicate?" in his *Philosophical Papers* (London: Allen & Unwin, 1959), pp. 145–76.
3. For a clear defense of such a view, compare Bertrand Russell's essay "On the Nature of Truth and Falsehood" in the first edition of his *Philosophical Essays* (London: Longmans, Green, 1919), pp. 170–85. Compare Russell's Introduction to the second edition of A. N. Whitehead and Bertrand Russell, *Principia Mathematica* (Cambridge: Cambridge University Press, 1935), pp. xvii–xxiii.

Chapter 5

1. 16b11. Quoted from J. L. Ackrill, ed., *Aristotle's Categories and De Interpretatione* (Oxford: Clarendon Press, 1963), pp. 44–5. Aristotle goes on to say, a few pages later: "An *affirmation* is a statement affirming something of something, a *negation* is a statement denying something of something" (17a25; Ackrill, p. 47).
2. Thomas Aquinas and Cardinal Cajetan, *Aristotle on Interpretation*, ed. Jean T. Oesterle (Milwaukee: Marquette University Press, 1962), p. 49.
3. See Bertrand Russell, *Introduction to Mathematical Philosophy* (London: Allen & Unwin, 1919), p. 179. For a more detailed discussion, see A. N. Whitehead and Bertrand Russell, *Principia Mathematica*, Vol. One, second edition (Cambridge: Cambridge University Press, 1935), pp. 173–85.
4. I add two points to prevent possible confusion. (a) Aristotle, in discussing *privation*, assumes that a member of a species can *fail to have* a property that is *essential* to the members of that species. A person who is blind would be an example. (b) Our ordinary language is not a reliable guide at this point. We say "x's properties have altered" when x's *states* are what have changed. This is somewhat like saying "The president's part changed" when a new president is inaugurated.

Chapter 6

1. See Ernest Sosa, "Propositional Attitudes *De Dicto* and *De Re*," *Journal of Philosophy*, Vol. LXVII (1970), pp. 883–96; W. V. Quine, "Quantifiers and Propositional Attitudes," in *The Ways of Paradox and Other Essays* (New York: Random House, 1966), pp. 183–94; David Kaplan, "Quantifying In," *Synthese*, Vol. XIX (1968), pp. 194–5; and Roderick M. Chisholm, *The First Person* (Minneapolis: University of Minnesota Press), chapter nine ("Knowledge and Belief *De Re*"), pp. 167–72.
2. See Ludwig Wittgenstein, *Philosophical Investigations* (Oxford: Basil Blackwell, 1956), p. 177.
3. See Hector-Neri Castañeda, "Practical Reasons for Doing and Intentional Action; and The Thinking of Doing and the Doing of Thinking," *Philosophical Perspectives*, Vol. IV (1990), pp. 273–308.
4. Philip E. B. Jourdain, *The Philosophy of Mr. Bertrand Russell* (London: Allen & Unwin, 1918), p. 34.
5. H. P. Grice, "Meaning," *Philosophical Review*, Vol. 66 (1957), pp. 377–88; the citation is from p. 385. This paper is included in Grice's *Studies in the Way of Words* (Cambridge, Mass.: Harvard University Press, 1989).
6. Compare A. N. Whitehead's example "This college building is commodious" in *The Concept of Nature* (Cambridge: Cambridge University Press, 1930), pp. 6–7. One corrects the speaker by making the true, but irrelevant, remark: "This is not a college building, it is the lion-house in the Zoo."
7. Immanuel Kant, *Lecture on Ethics* (New York: Harper & Row, 1963), p. 226.
8. See Anton Marty, *Untersuchungen zur Grundlegung der allgemeinen Grammatik und Sprachphilosophie* (Halle: Max Niemayer, 1909), p. 508.
9. Marty had said that in such cases the name is taken in the sense of "being what is named by this name [*in der Bedeutun des mit diesem Namen Genannten*]," ibid., p. 509.
10. Compare W. V. Quine's use of "purports to designate" in *Word and Object* (New York: John Wiley and Sons, 1960), chapter three.
11. The definition formulated there has a further clause designed to deal with Russell's paradox. That clause is not relevant to the present discussion.
12. Compare Wilfrid Sellars, "Intentionality and the Mental" in *Minnesota Studies in the Philosophy of Science* Vol. II (1957), pp. 507–39.

This article also contains a correspondence in which Sellars and I discuss these questions from opposing points of view.

Chapter 7

1. Compare the example in Rudolf Carnap, *The Logical Construction of the World* (Berkeley: University of California Press, 1963), pp. 63–4. This work first appeared in 1928.
2. Adapted from C. I. Lewis, *Survey of Symbolic Logic* (Berkeley: University of California Press, 1918), p. 119.
3. See p. 249 of Russell's "Mathematical Logic as Based on the Theory of Types," *American Journal of Mathematics,* Vol. XXX (1908), pp. 222–62. This is reprinted in *Essays on Logic and Knowledge* (London: Allen & Unwin, 1946), pp. 88–9. This material is included in *Principia Mathematica,* second edition (Cambridge: Cambridge University Press, 1935), pp. 71ff. and pp. 187ff.
4. Carnap's discussion of Russell's definition is in Rudolf Carnap, *Meaning and Necessity* (Chicago: University of Chicago Press, 1946), pp. 147–51.

Chapter 8

1. F. H. Bradley, *Appearance and Reality: A Metaphysical Study,* second edition (New York: Macmillan Co., 1902), pp. 24–34, 373–84. The quotation appears on p. 32n.
2. Kasimierz Kuratowski, "Sur la notion de l'ordre dans la théorie des Ensembles," *Fundamenta Mathematicae,* Vol. II (1921), pp. 161–71.
3. *Mathematical Logic* (New York: W. W. Norton and Co., 1940), p. 201. Compare Quine's *Word and Object* (New York: John Wiley and Sons, 1960), pp. 257ff. Quine remarks in *Word and Object* that "anyone who persists in recognizing intentional objects can take relations-in-intension . . . as attributes of ordered pairs" (p. 257n).

Chapter 9

1. A. N. Prior, *Papers on Time and Tense* (Oxford: Clarendon Press, 1968), p. 8.
2. Reprinted in Bertrand Russell, *Essays on Logic and Knowledge* (London: Allen & Unwin, 1946), pp. 347–63.
3. See *Essays on Logic and Knowledge,* pp. 347–63. There he notes that "for the mathematico-logical treatment of the subject, we need

only one fundamental relation, that of *wholly preceding*. . . . Two
events overlap, or are contemporaries, or are (at least partially)
simultaneous, if neither wholly precedes the other" (p. 347).

4. From the article "Calendar" in *Encyclopaedia Britannica*, Vol. VI
15th edition (Encyclopaedia Britannica Co.: 1974), pp. 595–612;
the quotation is from p. 595.

5. In the essay "On the Doctrine of the Indestructability of Our True
Nature by Death" in *The Wisdom of Life and Other Essays*, tr. Bailey
Saunders and E. B. Bax (Washington, D.C., and London: M. Wal-
ter Dunne, 1901), p. 308.

6. *Critique of Pure Reason*, B 46. See Norman Kemp Smith, ed., *Immanuel Kant's Critique of Pure Reason* (London: Macmillan & Co.,
1933), p. 74.

7. B 49; my italics. Kemp Smith, ed., *Immanuel Kant's Critique of Pure
Reason*, p. 76.

8. J. M. E. McTaggart, *The Nature of Existence*, Vol. II (Cambridge:
Cambridge University Press, 1927), pp. 9–31. The passages cited
here are from pp. 20 and 21.

9. The italics in (2') are mine.

10. See chapter 10, "Is There a 'Flow of Time' or Temporal Becom-
ing" of Adolf Grünbaum, *Philosophical Problems of Space and Time*
(New York: Alfred A. Knopf, 1963). The citation is from p. 316.
Compare his "The Status of Temporal Becoming" in Richard Gale,
ed., *The Philosophy of Time: A Collection of Essays* (New York and
London: Macmillan Co., 1968), pp. 322–54.

11. Grünbaum, "The Status of Temporal Becoming," p. 323.

Chapter 10

1. See Jaegwon Kim, "Events as Property Exemplifications,"
in Myles Brand and D. Wolton, ed., *Action Theory* (Dordrecht:
D. Reidel, 1976), pp. 159–77. The quotation appears on p. 160.
Compare the following article, also by Kim: "Causation, Nomic
Subsumption and Events," *Journal of Philosophy*, Vol. 70 (1973),
pp. 217–36.

2. Compare Lawrence Brian Lombard, *Events: A Metaphysical Study*
(London: Routledge & Kegan Paul, 1986), pp. 56–7, 77ff.

3. *Die Streit um die Existenz der Welt*, Vol. I (Tübingen: Max Niemayer
Verlag, 1864), p. 193.

4. Ibid., p. 193.

5. See, in particular, Kim, "Events as Property Exemplifications."

6. I am indebted to Johann C. Marek, who criticized an earlier version of this material.

7. F. W. Nietzsche, *The Will to Power*, Vol. IV (London: Allen & Unwin, Ltd., 1902), pp. 430–3.

8. At this point we ignore the possibility, suggested but not explicitly formulated by Bolzano, that we are eternal objects and hence that we did not come into being and will not pass away. It should be pointed out that although Bolzano was a priest, his views were seriously questioned by the authorities within the church. See Heinrich Fels, *Bernard Bolzano: Sein Leben und Sein Werk* (Leipzig: Felix Meiner Verlag, 1929), chapter three.

9. Compare the article "Causality" by Edward Madden in Hans Burkhardt and Barry Smith, eds., *Handbook of Metaphysics and Ontology*, Vol. I (Munich: Philosophia Verlag, 1992), pp. 133–36.

10. The general problem was first stated clearly by J. L. Mackie in "Causes and Conditions," *The American Philosophical Quarterly*, Vol. I (1965), pp. 245–64.

Chapter 11

1. *Generation and Corruption*, Book One, chapter 2 (316a). Quoted from the Oxford University Press translation. This passage is quoted from Richard McKeon, ed., *The Basic Words of Aristotle* (New York: Random House, 1941), p. 425.

2. *Exposition of Aristotle's Treatise on Generation and Corruption*, Part I, trans. by R. F. Larcher and Pierre Conway (Columbus: College of St. Mary of the Springs, 1964), Lecture IV, paragraph 29 (p. 13).

3. This analysis of the concept of a boundary is influenced by that of Brentano. The concept of a *state*, however, has no place in Brentano's general system.

4. The standard treatise on this subject is Peter Simons's *Parts: A Study in Ontology* (Oxford: Clarendon Press, 1987).

5. *The Physics*, Book IV, chapter 10. Compare W. D. Ross, *Aristotle* (London: Methuen & Co., 1937), pp. 31ff.

6. Franz Brentano, *Philosophical Investigations on Space, Time and the Continuum*, ed. by Stephan Körner and Roderick M. Chisholm and trans. by Barry Smith (London: Croom Helm, 1988). This book is a translation of *Philosophische Untersuchungen zu Raum, Qeit und Kontinuum* (Hamburg: Feliz Meiner Verlag, 1976).

7. See Gottlob Frege, *Grundgesetze der Arithmetik* (Jena: Verlag von Hermann Pohle, 1893), p. 59. Compare Frege's *The Foundations*

of Arithmetic with the German text, *Die Grundlagen der Arithmetik* (1884), translated by J. L. Austin (Oxford: Basil Blackwell, 1950), p. 92. The definition formulated here makes use of a simplification proposed by W. W. Quine in *Methods of Logic* (New York: Henry Holt and Co., 1959), p. 293. Quine's definition is, in turn, a simplification of the definition proposed in *Principia Mathematica*, Vol. I, second edition (Cambridge: Cambridge University Press, 1935), pp. 549ff.

8. I have discussed such entities in *Person and Object: A Metaphysical Study* (London: Allen & Unwin, 1976), pp. 148–58. Compare Peter Simons's discussion in *Parts*, pp. 187–95.

9. Compare Peter van Inwagen, *Material Beings* (Ithaca, N.Y.: Cornell University Press, 1990). Noting the importance of "the harmless-looking little word 'of,'" van Inwagen makes substantially the same distinction that is made here; see pp. 91ff. See Scott Hestevold, "Conjoining," *Philosophy and Phenomenological Research*, Vol. 41 (1980–81), pp. 371–83.

10. See W. V. Quine's discussion of the two senses of "Mary Had a Little Lamb" in *Word and Object* (New York: John Wiley and Sons, 1960), p. 90n. Compare C. J. Ducasse, *Nature, Mind and Death* (La Salle, Ill.: Open Court Publishing Co.), pp. 166ff.; F. D. Pelletier, *Mass Terms: Some Philosophical Problems* (Dordrecht: D. Reidel, 1979); and Helen Cartwright, "Parts and Partitives: Notes on What Things Are Made Of," *Synthese*, Vol. 58 (1984), pp. 251–77.

11. See Michio Kaka, *Hyperspace: A Scientific Odyssey through Parallel Universes* (New York: Oxford University Press, 1994).

12. David Kline and Carl A. Matheson, "The Impossibility of Collision," *Philosophy*, Vol. 62 (1987), pp. 509–15.

13. This is part of a more general argument about collision; that argument had as its first premise "A collision between two bodies involves their touching," and it drew the further conclusion that "Therefore no two bodies ever collide." Hence I have changed the numbering of the premises in this formulation. The additional problems that pertain to collision are not relevant to the present discussion.

14. It is quite possible that Kline and Matheson would accept this conclusion. In "The Impossibility of Collision" they write: "just as Descartes and Zeno can be seen as asking, 'Why are my premises false?' we can be seen as asking 'Why can material objects share regions of zero volume but not regions of non-zero volume?' Our remarks should be interpreted as a sceptical challenge – as a re-

quest for explanation – rather than as an attempt to make people refrain from bumping into each other" (p. 512).

15. For a discussion of some attempts to deal with this question in other ways, see Lawrence Brian Lombard, *Events: A Metaphysical Study* (London: Routledge, 1986), pp. 157ff.
16. Quoted by G. M. Duncan, in *The Philosophical Works of Leibniz* (New Haven, Conn.: Little, Morehouse & Taylor Co., 1909), pp. 334–5. The quotation is from chapter XXXVII, "The Letters to Samuel Clarke (1716)," pp. 328–480.
17. Ibid., p. 365.

Chapter 12

1. Immanuel Kant, *Critique of Pure Reason*, A351, from the translation by Norman Kemp Smith (London: Macmillan and Co., 1933), p. 335.
2. *Guide to the Perplexed* (London: Routledge and Kegan Paul, 1956), p. 143.
3. *Deskriptive Psychology*, ed. Roderick M. Chisholm and Wilhelm Baumgartner (Hamburg: Gelix Meiner Verlag, 1982), p. 11.

Chapter 13

1. We thus reject the adverbial theory of appearances. The classic discussion of the adverbial theory may be found in the articles by C. J. Ducasse and G. E. Moore in P. A. Schilpp, ed., *The Philosophy of G. E. Moore*, Vol. IV of *The Library of Living Philosophers* (Evanston, Ill.: Northwestern University Press, 1942). Ducasse's discussion ("Moore's Refutation of Idealism") appears on pp. 223–52. Moore's reply ("Subjectivity of Sense-Data") appears on pp. 653–60. See the article "Adverbial Theory," by Bruno Schuwey, in Hans Burkhardt and Barry Smith, eds., *Handbook of Metaphysics and Ontology* (Munich: Philosophia Verlag, 1992), pp. 18–20. In earlier writings, I defended the adverbial theory.
2. It may be recalled that we have taken "x is a constituent of y" as undefined and have, in effect, defined "x is part of y" as "x is a constituent of y, and x is not a boundary."
3. Thomas Case, *Physical Realism* (London: Longmans Green & Co., 1888), pp. 24–33.
4. I have set forth a detailed analysis in the third edition of *Theory*

of Knowledge (Englewood Cliffs, N.J., Prentice-Hall, 1989), pp. 39–48.

5. It has been questioned whether Fechner himself would accept the present version of the daylight view. See Leopold Stubenberg, "Chisholm, Fechner und das Leib-Seele Problem," in *Grazer Philosophische Studien*, Vol. 28 (1986), pp. 187–210. But as we have noted, the differences in philosophical terminology make it very difficult to compare the views of different philosophers who are concerned with this complex set of problems.

Chapter 14

1. *The Theaetetus*, 199a–b. From *The Dialogues of Plato*, 5 vols., ed. B. Jowett (Oxford: Oxford University Press, 1871).
2. St. Augustine, *The Anti-Pelagian Writings*, Vol. II (Edinburgh: T. & T. Clark, 1874), p. 323.
3. See E. S. Haldane and G. R. T. Ross, eds., *Philosophical Works of Descartes*, Vol. II (Cambridge: Cambridge University Press, 1934), pp. 9–10; compare pp. 52–3.
4. A. O. Lovejoy, *The Revolt against Dualism* (La Salle, Ill.: Open Court Press, 1930), p. 395.
5. Franz Brentano, *The Theory of Categories* (The Hague: Martinus Nijhoff, 1981), p. 18.
6. Rudolf Carnap, *The Logical Syntax of Language* (London: Routledge and Kegan Paul, 1937), p. 248.
7. See Gottlob Frege, "On Sense and Reference," in P. Geach and M. Black, eds., *Translations from the Philosophical Writings of Gottlob Frege* (Oxford: Basil Blackwell, 1952), pp. 56–78. I assume that Frege would say that the word *unicorn* has indirect reference in our intentional sentence. He defines *indirect reference* this way: "We distinguish . . . the *customary* from the *indirect* reference of a word; and its *customary* sense from its *indirect* sense. The indirect reference of a word is accordingly its customary sense" (p. 59).
8. Alonzo Church, *Introduction to Mathematical Logic* (Princeton, N.J.: Princeton University Press, 1955), p. 8n.

Chapter 15

1. We are not concerned here with that sense of "fictionalism," associated with Bentham and Vaihinger, according to which certain entities that are thought to exist and certain hypotheses that are

thought to be true are "merely useful fictions." See Arthur Fine, "Fictionalism," *Philosophical Perspectives*, Vol. XVIII (1994), pp. 1–18.

2. From the article "Fiction," by Kenneth L. Walton, in Hans Burkhardt and Barry Smith, eds., *Handbook of Metaphysics and Ontology*, Vol. I (Munich: Philosophia Verlag, 1991), pp. 274–5. The quotation is from p. 275. I have added "Sherlock" and the parenthetical expressions "(a)" through "(e)."

Chapter 16

1. *Philosophical Investigations on Space, Time and the Continuum*, ed. by Stephen Körner and R. Chisholm, trans. by Barry Smith (London: Croom Helm, 1988), p. 87. A number of other contemporary philosophers have adopted a similar view. Alvin Plantinga points out that the proposition expressed by "God is worshipped by St. Paul" was true at certain times and not at others. And from this he concludes that "it is surely clear that God does undergo change." Alvin Plantinga, *God and Other Minds* (Ithaca, N.Y.: Cornell University Press, 1962), p. 175. Compare Norman Kretzmann, "Omniscience and Immutability," *Journal of Philosophy*, Vol. 63 (1966), pp. 408–21; and the discussion of Kretzmann's paper in chapter nine ("God and Self-Knowledge: Omniscience and Indexical Reference") in Hector-Neri Castañeda, *Thinking and Experience* (Minneapolis: University of Minnesota Press, 1989), pp. 137–59. For a more detailed discussion of contemporary attempts to deal with this problem, see Edward Wierenga, *The Nature of God: An Inquiry into Divine Attributes* (Ithaca, N.Y.: Cornell University Press, 1993), pp. 166ff. Many of the philosophers to whom Wierenga refers seem to presuppose not only that there *are* such entities as times, but also that human beings are able to grasp the essences of times and then distinguish one time from another merely by reference to the essences of the two different times.

2. From Book V of *The Consolation of Philosophy*, as translated by Richard Green (Indianapolis, IN: The Bobbs-Merrill Co., Inc., 1962) p. 116.

3. See the *Summa Theologica* (New York: Benziger Brothers, 1947), First Part, Question 2 ("The Existence of God"), Article II ("Whether It Can Be Demonstrated That God Exists"). This material may be found on pp. 13–14 of Volume One of the three-volume edition of *The Summa Theologica* (1947). The same material, to-

gether with other relevant texts of St. Thomas, is also translated in Thomas Gilby, ed., *St. Thomas Aquinas: Philosophical Texts* (New York: Oxford University Press, 1960).

4. The translation is from the Benzinger edition, Vol. I, p. 14. Where the Benzinger version has "things which lack intelligence," Gilby has "things without consciousness"; where Benzinger has "not fortuitously but designedly," Gilby says, "by intention and not by chance"; and where Benzinger has "the best possible result," Gilby has "the best result"; for Benzinger's second use of "things without intelligence," Gilby has "things lacking knowledge."

5. *I Contra Gentes*, 42. Quoted by Gilby, *St. Thomas Aquinas*, p. 63.

6. Alvin Plantinga, *God and Other Minds* (Ithaca, N.Y.: Cornell University Press, 1967), p. 271.

7. The most thorough philosophical discussion of this concept of *function*, so far as I know, is found in Alvin Plantinga's *Warrant and Proper Function* (Oxford and New York: Oxford University Press, 1993). Pages 1–47 are particularly relevant to the present discussion.

INDEX

Ackrill, J. L., 133
Adamson, Robert, 133
addressing an utterance, 38–9
aggregates, 45–6
Aquinas, Thomas, 30, 86–7, 129–30,
  144
Aristotle, 3, 24, 29–31, 86
attributes, defined, 12; identity criteria for, 13–14; categorically open,
  29–30; negative, disjunctive and
  conjunctive, 31–3; oriented toward present, past, future, 57–8;
  recurrence of, 79; internal to substances, 75; internal to a thing,
  111
attributive sense, using words with,
  40
Augustine, 116
beginnings and endings, 74

Barcan, R. C., 133
Boethius, 128
Bolzano, Bernard, 139
boundaries, defined, 88; coincidence
  of, 90
Bradley, F. H., 51, 53–4
Brentano, Franz, 103, 117, 128, 139

Carnap, Rudolf, 48–9, 117–18, 137
Cartwright, Helen, 140
Case, Thomas, 110
Castañeda, Hector-Neri, 37, 143
causation, 80–2
Chisholm, R. M., 133, 136, 140,
  141–2
Church, Alonzo, 118
classes, 45–9
conceptual entailment, defined, 12

content of an act of believing, 6, 11
contingent things, defined, 17
Cresswell, M. J., 133
critical commonsensism, 4

demonstratives, 39–40
de re belief, 35–6
Descartes, Rene, 116
Ducasse, C. J., 140, 141

endeavor, 119
entia necessarium, defined, 17; 61
events, defined, 77; parts of, 83
extreme realism, 4, 21

facts, defined, 25
Fine, Arthur, 143
Frege, Gottlob, 139–40, 142

Galileo, Galilei, 91
Grice, H. P., 38
Grünbaum, Adolf, 68–9

Hestevold, Scott, 140
Hughes, G. E., 133

implication, a relation between attributes, 75
Ingarden, Roman, 73–4
intentional inexistence, 115

Jourdain, P. E. B., 37

Kaka, Michio, 140
Kant, Immanuel, 24, 66–7, 100–1
Kaplan, David, 136
Kim, Jaegwon, 71, 77
Kline, David, 95–6